Houghton Mifflin Science

DISCOVERYWORKS

 HOUGHTON MIFFLIN

Boston • Atlanta • Dallas • Denver • Geneva, Illinois • Palo Alto • Princeton

Authors

William Badders
Elementary Science Teacher
Cleveland Public Schools
Cleveland, OH

Lowell J. Bethel
Professor of Science Education
The University of Texas at Austin
Austin, TX

Victoria Fu
Professor of Child Development
and Early Childhood Education
Virginia Polytechnic Institute and
State University
Blacksburg, VA

Donald Peck
Director (retired)
The Center for Elementary Science
Fairleigh Dickinson University
Madison, NJ

Carolyn Sumners
Director of Astronomy and Physical Sciences
Houston Museum of Natural Science
Houston, TX

Catherine Valentino
Author-in-Residence, Houghton Mifflin
West Kingston, RI

Acknowledgements appear on page H28, which
constitutes an extension of this copyright page.

Printed in the U. S. A.

ISBN-13:978-0-618-16750-0
ISBN-10:0- 618-16750-1

9 10 DW 10 09 08 07

CONTENTS

THINK LIKE A SCIENTIST

FLOATING AND SINKING

A scientist thinks about ideas in a careful way. You too, can think like a scientist.

Observe

To think like a scientist, **observe** the things around you. Everything you hear and see is a clue about how the world works.

Roland and Shannon are playing with clay. They make the clay into many shapes. Roland places a clay ball into water. The clay ball sinks. Why did this happen?

Ask a Question

As you observe, you may see that some things happen over and over. **Ask questions** about such things.

Roland says that the clay ball is too heavy to float. Shannon points out that heavy boats float. How can Roland and Shannon change the clay so it will float?

Make a Hypothesis

Suppose you have an idea about why something happens. You make a **hypothesis**, or a guess based on your idea.

Shannon has an idea about what made the clay ball sink. She thinks that changing the shape of the clay might make the clay float. What do you think?

Plan and Do a Test

After you make a hypothesis, **plan** how to **test** it. Then carry out your plan.

Roland and Shannon test the idea.
Roland makes the clay ball into a boat.
The boat has space inside it. He puts
the boat in water. Will it float?

Record What Happens

You need to observe your test carefully. Then **record**, or write down, what happens.

Roland and Shannon watch the clay boat. They see that it floats. Shannon records what they did and what happened. What did she write?

Draw Conclusions

Think about reasons why something happened as it did. Then **draw conclusions**.

Roland decides that the shape of the boat and the space inside help it float. The clay ball did not have a space inside and so the ball could not float. Try it!

READING TO LEARN

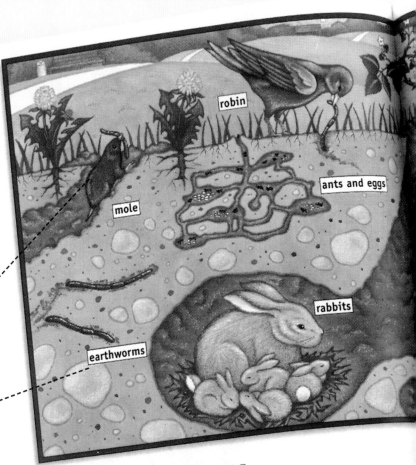

Before You Read

1. **Look** at the pictures.

2. **Read** the words.

3. **Read** the title.

4. **Look** at the **new words**.

robin

mole

ants and eggs

rabbits

earthworms

Underground Homes

All animals need a **shelter**. A shelter is a place where an animal can rest and be safe. It protects the animal from heat and cold. It is a place to store food. It is also where animals take care of their young. Shelters can be made with living and nonliving things. Shelters can be in many places.

A22   INTERACTIONS OF LIVING THINGS

Scientists read to have fun and to learn.
You can, too! Just follow these steps.

chipmunk

Look at the picture. Some animals dig into the soil to make their homes. The mother rabbit puts grass in her shelter to make a soft nest for her young.

The chipmunk stores acorns in a hole. The ants lay eggs in tunnels. The earthworms find food in the soil. All these animals make their homes underground.

Reading Check Write about the shelter for an animal you know. What makes it a good shelter?

LESSON 5 RESOURCE A23

While You Read

1. **Read** the words carefully.

2. **Look** at the pictures again.

3. **Ask** for help if you need it.

After You Read

1. **Tell** what you have learned.

2. **Show** what you have learned.

SAFETY

Wear your goggles when your teacher tells you.

Handle materials carefully.

Never put things into your mouth.

Wash your hands after every activity.

Always tell an adult if you are hurt.

Be kind to living things.

Clean up spills.

Recycle

Soil

Save resources and materials to use again.

Throw out materials you can't use again.

UNIT A

Interactions Of Living Things

Themes: Constancy and Change; Models

How are living and nonliving things different?

Activity

Classifying Objects

What You Need

 hand lens

 empty paper bag

 bag of woodland objects

 Science Notebook

1 **Collect** objects from the schoolyard. Put them in a bag.

Nonliving

2 **Sort** the objects into two groups. Put living and once-living in one group. Put nonliving in another group. **Record** each group of objects in a chart.

Sorting Objects		
Schoolyard Objects	Living or Once-Living	Nonliving

3 Repeat step 2, using woodland objects.

4 Use a hand lens to **observe** the groups of objects. **Compare** woodland objects with schoolyard objects.

Think! How did you decide which objects to put in each group?

Living or Once-Living

Living and Nonliving Things

Imagine being in this woodland. How might you classify the things around you? You could classify them as living, once-living, or nonliving things.

A **living thing** needs food, water, and air. It can grow. A living thing can also make new living things. Plants and animals are living things.

saw-whet owl

painted turtle

Once-living things are not living now. What things in the picture were living in the past? Dead leaves, logs, and broken twigs are once-living things.

Nonliving things have never needed food, water, or air. They have not grown. They have not made new living things. Rocks are nonliving things.

Reading Check Draw a picture of some living, once-living, and nonliving things. How are they different?

What do living things need?

Activity
Making a Terrarium

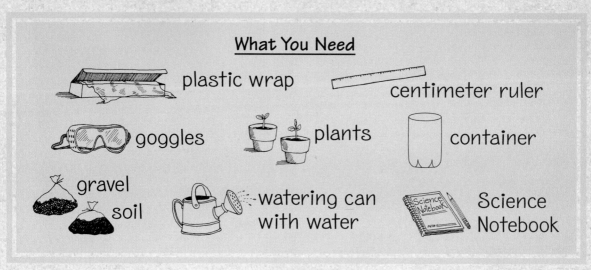

What You Need

plastic wrap   centimeter ruler

goggles   plants   container

gravel
soil   watering can   Science
          with water   Notebook

1 **Using Math** In a container, put gravel about 3 centimeters deep.

2 Cover the gravel with soil about 7 centimeters deep.

3 Add water to the soil. Put plants into the soil. Then cover the terrarium.

4 **Talk about** how to care for your terrarium. **Record** your plan.

Think! How do living things in the terrarium get what they need?

Find Out More!

How could animals use this habitat? Ask questions. Add some animals. Tell about what you observe.

Living Things Have Needs

A **habitat** is the home of a living thing. In a habitat, plants and animals get what they need to live.

The first picture shows a desert habitat. There is food, air, and light for the living things. There is not much water. Desert plants and animals can live where there is very little water.

The second picture shows a seacoast habitat. It has food, air, light, and a lot of salty water. Some plants and animals need salty water to live.

The picture shows colorful sea stars. Sea stars, or starfish, eat other animals. The sea star gets its food and other things it needs from its seacoast habitat.

Reading Check Pretend you are an animal. **Tell a story** about where you live and what you need to live.

How do plant parts help a plant?

Activity
Observing Roots

What You Need

 hand lens

 tweezers

 tray with seedlings on a paper towel

 Science Notebook

1 Use a hand lens to **observe** seedlings. **Talk about** what the roots look like. **Draw** what you see.

2 Carefully turn the paper towel upside down and shake gently. **Record** what happens.

3 Gently try to pull a seedling off the towel. **Observe** the roots closely while you do this. **Record** what happens.

Think! How do roots help a plant to survive?

dandelion

Parts of Plants

A plant needs food, water, air, and light to live. Plant parts help a plant get food, water, and air from its habitat. Most plants get light from the sun.

Look at the picture of the dandelion. It has one thick root and many smaller roots that go deep into the soil. It has stems that lead to flat leaves.

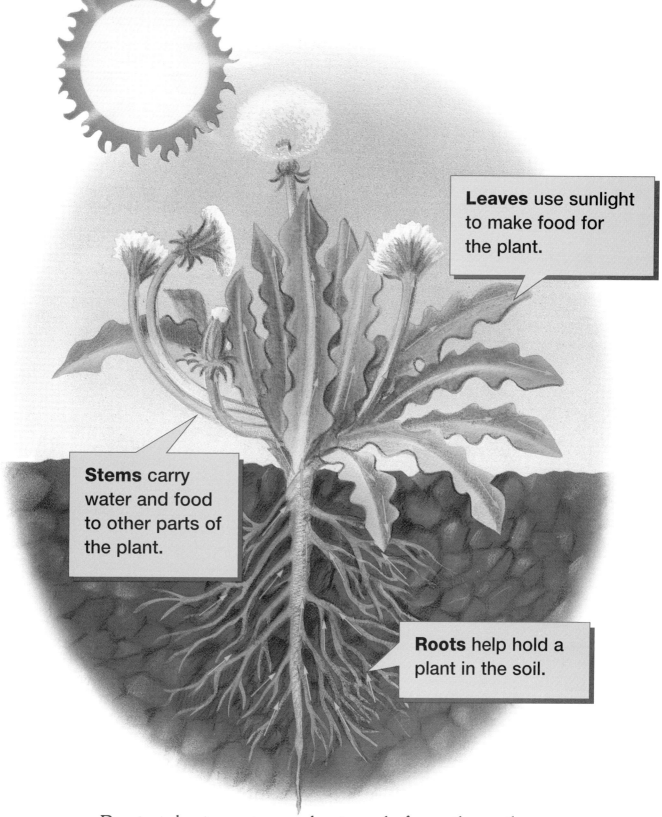

Roots take in water and minerals from the soil. Water and minerals move from the roots to the stems to the leaves. Follow the arrows to see how water moves through the plant.

prickly pear cactus

Look at the picture of the cactus. What parts do you see? In what ways are the cactus and the dandelion alike? In what ways are they different?

Both plants have roots, stems, and leaves. The cactus has tiny, sharp leaves called **spines**. The cactus lives mainly in the desert, where there is little rain. Plants with spines lose less water than plants with flat leaves.

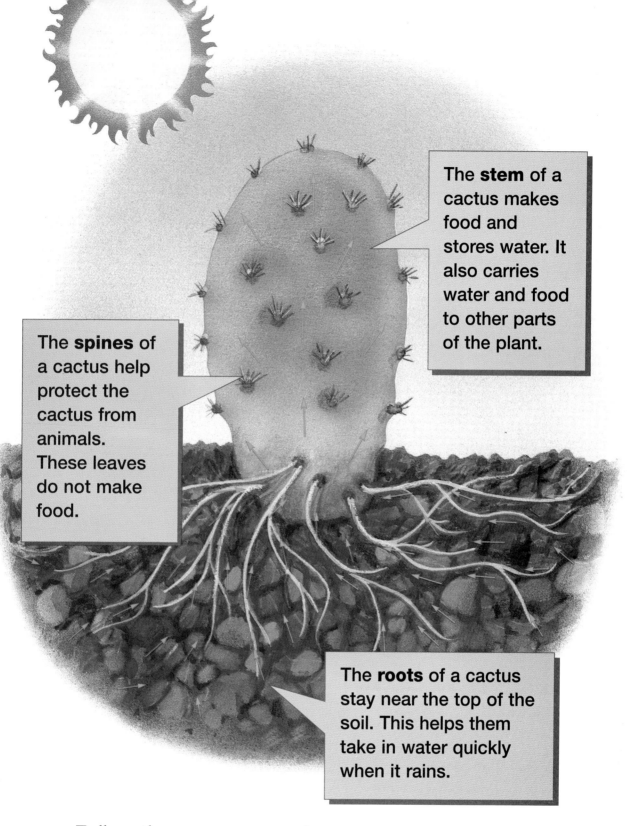

The **stem** of a cactus makes food and stores water. It also carries water and food to other parts of the plant.

The **spines** of a cactus help protect the cactus from animals. These leaves do not make food.

The **roots** of a cactus stay near the top of the soil. This helps them take in water quickly when it rains.

Follow the arrows to see how water moves through the cactus.

Reading Check Write about how the parts of a cactus or a dandelion help the plant to live.

LESSON 4

How do living things use their habitats?

Activity
Using Resources

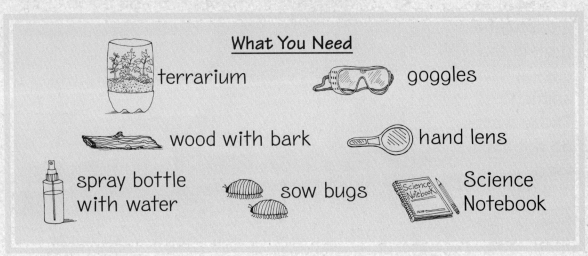

What You Need

terrarium

goggles

wood with bark

hand lens

spray bottle with water

sow bugs

Science Notebook

1 Use a hand lens to **observe** a sow bug. **Draw** what you see.

2 **Predict** where sow bugs will go when you put them in a terrarium. Put them in and **record** what happens.

3 Spray a piece of wood with water. Put the wood in the terrarium.

4 Move a sow bug to a dry spot in the terrarium. Cover the terrarium. **Record** what the sow bug does. **Talk about** why you think it does this.

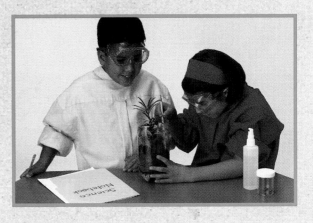

Think! How does a sow bug use the terrarium to meet its needs?

Internet Field Trip

Visit **www.eduplace.com** to see how animals use their habitats.

Meeting Needs

This habitat is a swamp. Birds and other animals live here. How is a swamp different from a desert or a woodland? Water covers the land most of the time.

Many plants live in a swamp. Most of the plants are trees. The picture shows bald cypress trees. Their roots stay near the top of the water.

The American alligator lives in the swamps of the southern United States.

Things that plants and animals use to live are called **resources**. This alligator needs living things in the swamp. It eats frogs, birds, and other animals.

An alligator also uses nonliving things to live. These things include air, light, and water. What other resources in the swamp might an animal use to live?

> ✅ **Reading Check Write a story** about an animal and how it uses the resources in its habitat.

LESSON 5

Where do animals find shelter?

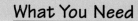

Activity
Observing Animal Shelters

What You Need

 craft materials

 hand lens

 Science Notebook

1 Take a walk around the schoolyard with your class. Look for animals.

2 **Observe** some animals in their habitats. **Record** the kinds of shelters you see.

Observing Animal Shelters	
Animal	Kind of Shelter

3 **Make a model** of one of the shelters you saw.

Think! How are the shelters you observed like other animal shelters you know?

Underground Homes

All animals need a **shelter**. A shelter is a place where an animal can rest and be safe. It protects the animal from heat and cold. It is a place to store food. It is also where animals take care of their young.

Shelters can be made with living and nonliving things. Shelters can be in many places.

chipmunk

Look at the picture. Some animals dig into the soil to make their homes. The mother rabbit puts grass in her shelter to make a soft nest for her young.

The chipmunk stores acorns in a hole. The ants lay eggs in tunnels. The earthworms find food in the soil. All these animals make their homes underground.

> **Reading Check** **Write** about the shelter for an animal you know. What makes it a good shelter?

How do body parts help an animal?

Activity
Eating Like a Bird

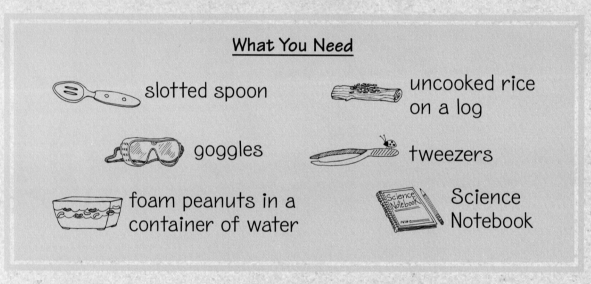

What You Need

slotted spoon

uncooked rice on a log

goggles

tweezers

foam peanuts in a container of water

Science Notebook

1. Pretend each tool is a bird's mouth and the peanuts and rice are bird food.

2. Use each tool to pick up a piece of rice.

3. Use each tool to pick up some foam peanuts.

4 Which mouth worked better to pick up each kind of food? **Record** your findings.

Think! Why was one type of mouth better for picking up some kinds of foods?

Fish in the water

Bugs on a log

ibis ▶

▲ common
moorhen

northern
shoveler ▶

Animal Body Parts

Animals have body parts that help them live. A
beak is a mouth part that helps a bird get food.

Some birds have scooping beaks that are also
called **bills**. The moorhen and the northern shoveler
are birds that live in water and eat plants. They use
their bills to scoop plants out of the water.

downy woodpecker

Atlantic puffin ▼

▲ toco toucan

Some birds have beaks that are used to pick up things like seeds or nuts. The long beak of the ibis is used to spear fish or frogs in shallow water. The toucan carries eggs in its beak.

The woodpecker uses its beak to drill through nuts and bark to get food. The puffin catches fish in its beak. Then it carries the fish back to its nest. A puffin can gobble up many small fish.

Animals use different body parts to get food.
These animals use their legs to help them get food.

◄ The eagle has talons, or claws, on its feet. It uses these to grasp fish.

The crab has five pairs of legs. The front pair of legs has claws that it uses to get food. ▼

▲ The giraffe uses its long neck and long legs to reach the leaves at the tops of trees.

INTERACTIONS OF LIVING THINGS

◄ The water strider uses its four back legs to stay on top of the water. It uses its two shorter front legs to catch food.

The tarantula uses its eight legs to walk and climb to catch insects. ▶

Using Math Make a chart like the one shown. Complete the chart to show the number of legs that each animal has.

Animal Legs					
Animal	eagle	giraffe	water strider	tarantula	crab
Number of Legs	2				

Tell what pattern you see.

Reading Check Choose two animals to compare. **Tell** how they use their body parts to get their food.

Word Power

If you need help, turn to the pages shown in blue.

Match the words with a plant part. (A12–A15)

roots   stems   leaves

1.    **2.** → 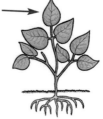   **3.** →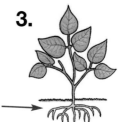

Use these words to fill in the blanks.

once-living things   habitat
nonliving things   spines

4. Things that have never needed food, water, or air are _____. (A4–A5)

5. A home for a living thing is a _____. (A8–A9)

6. The sharp leaves of a cactus are called _____. (A14–A15)

7. Things that were living in the past but are not living now are _____. (A4–A5)

Solving Science Problems

Make a chart like the one shown. Decide what living, once-living, and nonliving things you will add to your chart. Tell why you decided to add each thing.

Living Things	Once-Living Things	Nonliving Things
trees	dead leaves	rocks

People Using Science

Greenhouse Gardener

A greenhouse is a place where plants are grown. Greenhouse gardeners care for the plants. They plant seeds to grow new plants.

The gardeners put the plants in pots of soil. They give each plant water and food.

Look at the picture. Why do you think plants grow well in a greenhouse?

 ## Using a Table

Sprouting Seeds							
Day	Sun.	Mon.	Tues.	Wed.	Thurs.	Fri.	Sat.
Number of Seeds	10	25	19	17	23	14	8

Use the table to answer the questions.

1. How many seeds sprouted on Wednesday?

2. On which day did the most seeds sprout?

3. How many seeds sprouted on Sunday and Thursday altogether?

4. How many more seeds sprouted on Friday than on Saturday?

Why do animals change their habitats?

Activity
Building a Beaver Dam

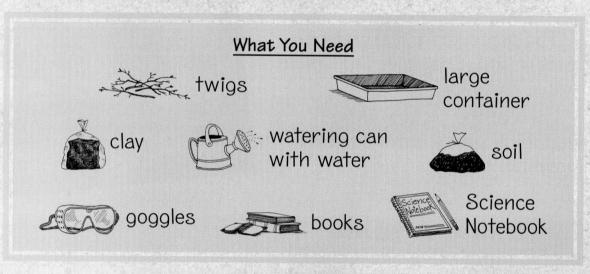

What You Need

twigs

large container

clay

watering can with water

soil

goggles

books

Science Notebook

1 Cover the bottom of a container with soil. Make a riverbed down the center with your fingers.

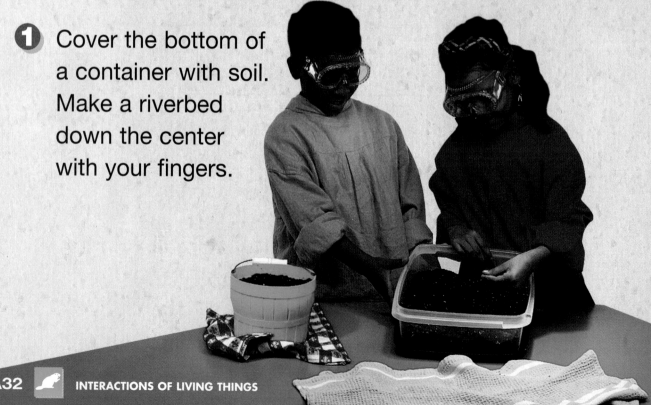

2 Build a dam by twisting twigs together. Pack any holes in the dam with clay.

3 Place some books under one end of the container. Place the dam across the riverbed.

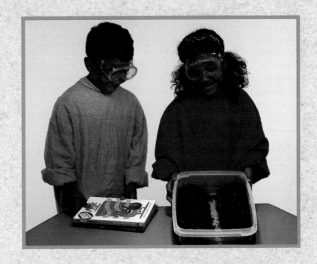

4 **Predict** what will happen when you pour water down the riverbed. Pour water slowly and **record** what you see.

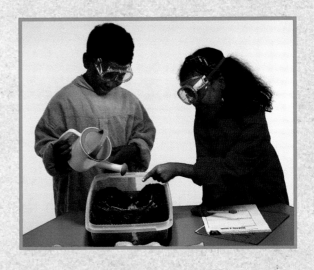

Think! Why does a beaver build a dam?

Changing the Habitat

Some animals make changes to their habitats. A **beaver** is one such animal. It uses its teeth to cut down trees. Look at the tree that the beaver is cutting. The tree will fall across the river. This is the start of a **beaver dam**. The beaver dam will cross the **riverbed** from one side to the other to stop the water.

The three small photos show a beaver at work.
First, the beaver uses its sharp teeth to cut down
trees. Next, it carries twigs in its mouth through the
water. The beaver uses its legs, feet, and tail to swim.
Last, its paddle-shaped tail helps the beaver pack
twigs, stones, and mud around the fallen trees.

Turn the page. See how the woodland looks after
the beaver builds its dam.

The beaver has built the dam. A pond has formed behind it. The pond is a place of still water. Here the beaver builds its shelter.

The beaver's shelter is called a **lodge**. A beaver lodge is made of the same things the beaver used for the dam—trees, twigs, mud, and stones. A beaver stays warm and stores food in its lodge. The lodge is also a place where the beaver raises its young.

Some termites build large nests with bits of soil. The nests can be 6 meters (20 feet) tall.

Black-tailed prairie dogs build burrows. These are safe places to raise their young.

Other animals also change their habitats. Prairie dogs dig long tunnels. Termites build large nests above ground. What other changes do animals make?

Some changes that animals make hurt others. When beavers cut down trees, some animals lose their homes. Cattle can step in holes that prairie dogs dig.

> ✔ **Reading Check Act out a story** to show an animal changing its habitat to meet its needs.

What causes changes in an environment?

Activity
Washing Away the Land

What You Need

 pan with soil in it

 pan with soil and plants in it

 towels

 books

 goggles

 watering can with water

 Science Notebook

1 Make a hill by putting books under one end of a pan with soil in it.

2 Place a towel under the lower end of the pan. Pour water down the hill. **Record** what happens.

3 Put books under one end of a pan with plants in it. **Predict** what you think will happen when you pour water down this hill.

4 Repeat step 2, using the pan with the plants in it.

Think! How do plants affect the flow of water down a hill?

Find Out More!

What other things might affect the flow of water? Make a plan to test your ideas. Share your results with your classmates.

More Changes

An **environment** is the area around a living
thing. It includes all of the living and nonliving things
in the area. People can change an environment.
Natural forces can also cause changes.

Look at the picture. What changes are people
making? What changes are being made by nature?

Changes can be both helpful and harmful. How are people helping and harming this area?

Planting trees and picking up trash are helpful. Building a road or a house can be harmful. Cutting down trees can cause erosion. **Erosion** is the washing away of land. The roots of trees hold soil in place. Roots can help stop erosion. Think of other things that people do that help or harm an area.

Trash dumped in water ▶

Forest fires are helpful when they clear away leaves and dead trees. Forest fires are harmful when they kill living things. They also are harmful when they destroy the homes of living things.

Dumping trash into a pond or river is harmful. The trash pollutes the water. People cannot use the water. Fish and other animals cannot live in the water. The water is not safe for animals to drink.

▲ **Replanting trees**

Sometimes trees are harmed by volcanoes.
Sometimes trees are harmed by lightning or fire.
Sometimes people cut down trees.

People can plant new trees to take their place.
New trees will help hold soil in place. Animals can
make homes in the new trees.

Reading Check **Draw a picture** to show how
people can change the environment.

What lives in a desert habitat?

Activity
Making a Desert Garden

What You Need

small cactuses

aloe

gravel and soil

watering can with water

bowl

centimeter ruler

hand lens

gardening gloves

goggles

Science Notebook

1 Using Math In a bowl, put gravel about 2 centimeters deep. Spread soil about 5 centimeters deep over the gravel.

2 Break off a piece of aloe. **Observe** the inside of the plant. **Record** what you see.

3 Be careful of the spines. Put the plants into the soil. Water the plants just a little.

4 **Talk about** how to care for your desert garden. **Record** your plan.

Think! What would happen to these plants if you watered them too much?

Internet Field Trip

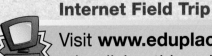

Visit **www.eduplace.com** to see other living things in the desert.

Living in the Desert

Desert plants and animals need food, water, air, and light. A desert gets very little rain. Desert plants and animals can live with very little water.

A cactus stores water in its stem. It looks fatter with water in it. The desert tortoise uses the cactus to get water. It uses desert plants to get food.

red-tailed hawk

desert tortoise

Some animals use plants for shelter. The hawks in the picture made their nest in a cactus. The high nest protects the baby birds from other animals.

In the desert, the days are very hot and the nights are cold. The tortoise digs a deep nest in the sand. Why is this a good place for a nest?

> **Reading Check Draw a picture** of a desert plant or animal. How can it live in the desert?

LESSON 10

Why do different things live in different habitats?

Activity
Comparing Habitats

What You Need

 desert garden   hand lens

 woodland terrarium   Science Notebook

1 Use a hand lens to **observe** the plants and soil in each habitat. **Record** how they are alike and different.

Comparing Habitats	
Alike	**Different**

  INTERACTIONS OF LIVING THINGS

2 **Talk about** what would happen to a woodland plant if you put it in the desert garden.

3 **Talk about** what would happen to a desert plant if you put it in the woodland environment.

Think! If all plants need water, how can some plants live where it is dry?

Find Out More!

CD-ROM

Use **Science Blaster**™ **Jr.** to compare sizes of living things. Compare a beech tree and a redwood tree. Compare a whale and a shark.

The polar bear lives where it is cold and snowy.

Some Other Habitats

Plants and animals live in different places. Many animals cannot live in the desert. It is too warm and dry for a polar bear. It is too dry for a flamingo.

What helps a polar bear live in the Arctic? It has thick fur that helps keep it warm. Its fur looks white. This color helps a polar bear hide on ice and snow.

The American flamingo lives where it is warm and wet.

What helps a flamingo live in wet places? Its long legs help it wade in water. Its bill helps it scoop food out of the water and scoop mud for a nest.

Plants that live where the flamingo does could not live in the Arctic. It is too cold there. Can desert plants live in the Arctic? Tell why or why not.

Reading Check **Tell a story** about an animal. Where does it live? What helps it live where it does?

UNIT A

UNIT REVIEW

Word Power

If you need help, turn to the pages shown in blue.

Match the words with a picture. (A4–A5)

living thing   once-living thing   nonliving thing

1.   **2.**   **3.**

Write the letter of the correct word.

4. A _____ helps a bird pick up food. (A26–A27)
  a. neck   **b.** wing   **c.** beak   **d.** tongue

5. Plants and animals use _____ to live. (A18–A19)
  a. trash   **b.** erosion   **c.** spines   **d.** resources

6. The washing away of soil is _____. (A40–A41)
  a. roots   **b.** shelter   **c.** dam   **d.** erosion

7. The parts of a plant that carry food and water to other parts are the _____. (A12–A15)
  a. stems   **b.** roots   **c.** leaves   **d.** flowers

8. _____ protect cactuses from animals. (A14–A15)
  a. Stems   **b.** Roots   **c.** Spines   **d.** Flowers

9. A beaver builds a home called a _____. (A36–A37)
  a. dam   **b.** lodge   **c.** swamp   **d.** nest

10. Animals can rest and raise young in a _____. (A22–A23)
  a. shelter   **b.** resource   **c.** dam   **d.** spine

Using Science Ideas

How many living things can you find in this woodland habitat? List them.

Writing in Science

Make a chart like the one shown. Add more living things. Then complete your chart. Explain why the living thing lives in the habitat and how the special features help it live there. Then write about one of the animals.

Living Thing	Habitat	Special Features
polar bear	Arctic	thick, white fur

Compare and Contrast

Katie made a chart to compare two animals. She thought about questions that would help her.

	Robin	Giraffe
Where do they live?	Lives in a woodland or city park	Lives on the savanna in Africa
What do they eat?	Eats worms, insects, and berries	Eats parts of trees and grass
How do they move?	Flies and walks	Walks

Choose two animals that you have learned about. Think about how they are alike and different. Make a chart to compare them the way Katie did.

Using MATH SKILLS

 Make a Bar Graph

Mrs. Brown's class took a trip to the zoo. They made a chart to show the number of animals they saw in each habitat.

Animals in Each Habitat

Habitat	Tally	Total
Woodland	卌 I	6
Swamp	III	3
Desert	卌	5
Seacoast	IIII	4

Make a bar graph like the one shown below. Color one box for each animal in each habitat.

Animals in Each Habitat

6
5
4
3
2
1
0

Woodland   Swamp   Desert   Seacoast

Use the graph to answer each question.

1. Which habitat has the most animals?

2. How many more animals are in the woodland than in the swamp?

3. How many fewer animals are in the seacoast than in the desert?

4. What is the total number of animals shown on the graph?

UNIT B

Energy and Motion

Themes: Constancy and Change; Scale

LESSON 1

How does light move?

Activity

Observing the Path of Light

What You Need

flashlight   construction paper

mirror   crayons   Science Notebook

1 Darken the room. Shine a flashlight across a sheet of paper.

2 Try to make the light curve or bend. **Record** what happens.

3 Have a partner hold a mirror on the paper. Make the light hit the mirror. **Record** what you see.

4 Change the position of the mirror. **Record** what you see.

Think! How can you change the direction of light?

Internet Field Trip

Visit **www.eduplace.com** to find out more about light.

Light on the Move

What fun it is to play flashlight tag! In this game, the person who is "it" shines a flashlight to tag another child. Think about how light moves. Where could you hide so that you don't get tagged? You might hide behind a tree. A tree blocks the path of **light**. The light cannot turn to go around the tree.

The light moves in straight lines until it hits an object. That's why you can point a flashlight at others and tag them with the light. You can't tag someone who is behind a tree.

How does light get from the porch light to the book? Light moves away from the bulb in all directions. Some of the light shines on the pages of the book. What are other objects light shines on?

Suppose you play flashlight tag again. This time, you are "it" and you have a partner. You want to tag a child behind a rock. How can you work together?

You can give your partner a mirror. Then you shine the flashlight at the mirror. The mirror **reflects** light. The light bounces off the mirror and moves in a new direction. Now the light shines behind the rock. The child is tagged!

A mirror reflects light. So do other objects. Light from the porch light hits the book. The pages of the book reflect some of the light. The light changes direction. The light keeps moving in straight lines to shine on the man's face. What else in the picture is reflecting light?

Reading Check Draw a picture to show how light can go around a corner.

What things let light pass through?

Activity

Observing Light as It Strikes Objects

What You Need

cup of water

cup of milky water

3 kinds of paper

flashlight

3 kinds of food wrap

mirror

Science Notebook

1 **Predict** whether all light, some light, or no light will pass through the objects. **Record** your predictions.

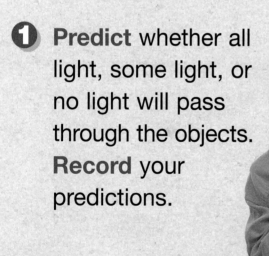

2 Darken the room. Shine a flashlight through a cup of clear water. **Record** what happens to the light.

3 Shine light through the other objects. **Record** what happens.

4 **Compare** your predictions with your observations.

Think! How are the objects that do not let light pass through them alike?

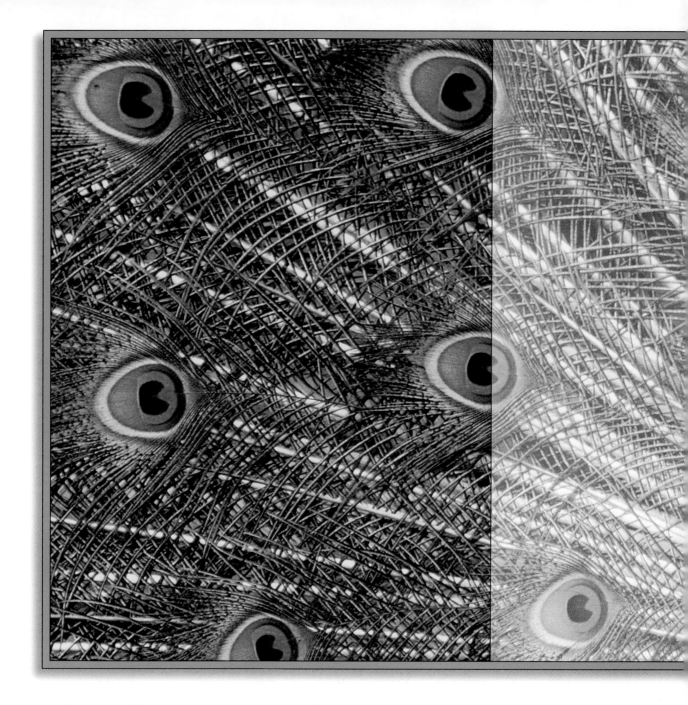

Can You See the Light?

Light passes through some objects. These objects are **transparent**. Some objects let a little light through. They are **translucent**. Other objects let no light pass through. These objects are **opaque**.

This picture has three coverings. Which one is opaque? Which is transparent? Which is translucent?

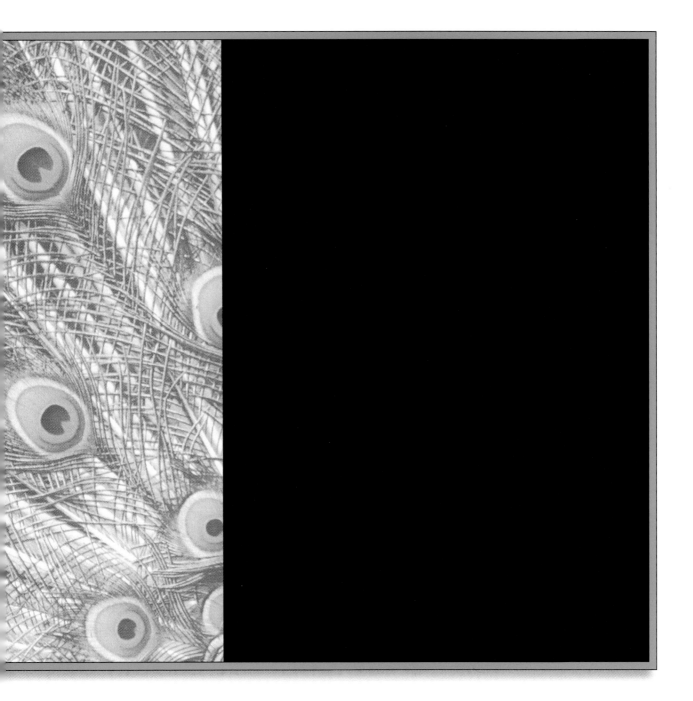

Think of other places you can *see* different coverings. Suppose you are helping to pack your lunch. You wrap your sandwich in a piece of wax paper. The sandwich looks blurred. That's because wax paper is translucent.

Suppose you put your sandwich in a wrap that is opaque. You might use aluminum foil or brown paper. What kind of wrap is transparent?

Look at the picture now. The coverings have been removed. You can see what was under the opaque and translucent coverings.

The transparent covering was clear. When it covered the picture, you could still see what was under it. What other things are transparent? Think of things you can see through. You might think of a window, clear water, or the air around you.

Suppose you are sitting at home at your desk. You hold up a ball in front of the lamp. The ball is opaque. It blocks the light and makes a **shadow**.

You are opaque, too. Stand in front of a light. Face away from the light. Look at your shadow. Wiggle your arms. How does your shadow change?

Reading Check Make lists of things that are transparent, translucent, and opaque.

LESSON 3
How do lenses change light?

Activity
Exploring Lenses

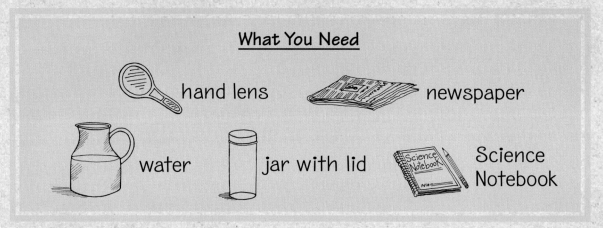

What You Need

hand lens   newspaper

water   jar with lid   Science Notebook

1 Fill a jar with water. Put the lid on tightly.

2 Look through the jar at a piece of newspaper. **Observe** and **record** how the letters and words look.

3 Move the jar away from you and back toward you. **Describe** how the letters seem to change.

4 Repeat steps 2–3, using a hand lens. **Compare** what you see through the hand lens with what you saw through the jar of water.

Think! How are a jar of water and a hand lens alike?

Light Through Lenses

A container filled with water is curved and transparent. It is a kind of **lens**. When light strikes a lens, the light passes through. However, the light bends. The light moves in a new direction. Objects you see through a lens look different. Lenses can make objects look bigger or smaller.

There are many kinds of lenses in the picture. A pair of eyeglasses has two lenses. The hand lens has one. People and fish have a lens in each eye.

The water in the tank acts like a lens. It makes the handle of the net look bigger. Where else have you seen lenses change how something looks?

✔ **Reading Check** **Write** about how lenses change the way you see an object.

How do you know when something moves?

Activity
Measuring Motion

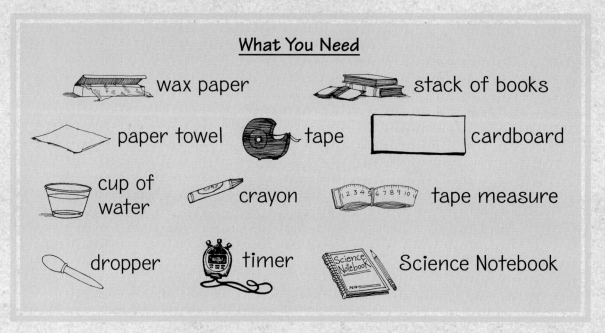

What You Need

wax paper　　　　stack of books

paper towel　　tape　　cardboard

cup of water　　crayon　　tape measure

dropper　　timer　　Science Notebook

1 Use a crayon to draw a starting line on the cardboard. Tape wax paper onto the cardboard.

2 Make a pile of books about 10 centimeters high. Put the starting end of the cardboard on the books to make a ramp.

3 Place a drop of water on the starting line. Time the drop for 4 seconds. Mark and **measure** how far the drop moved. **Record** your measurement.

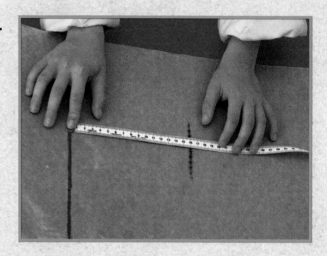

4 Use a paper towel to blot the water. Then repeat step 3. This time, **measure** how far the drop moves in 8 seconds. **Compare** the distances.

Measuring Motion	
Time	**Distance**
4 seconds	
8 seconds	

Think! What differences do you see in the two measurements? Why?

Things in Motion

A runner pushes off the starting blocks. A racecar zooms around a track. A flying disk sails through the air. A speed skater glides along an icy track. What do these things have in common?

They are all things in **motion**. When something is in motion, it changes its position.

What are some ways to measure motion? You can measure the distance something has traveled. Then you will know how far it has moved.

You can also use a stopwatch to measure how much time it took. A racecar can go more than three miles in one minute. That's a fast **speed**!

Reading Check Tell how you know when something has moved.

LESSON 5

What causes changes in motion?

Activity
Exploring Pushes

What You Need

index card

marble

book

Science Notebook

1 Make two folds along an index card. Place one end of the card on a book to make a ramp on the floor.

2 Hold a marble at the top of the ramp. Let it go. **Observe** the direction it moves across the floor.

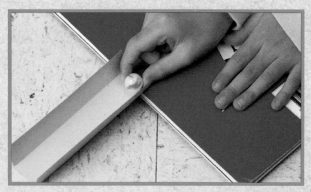

3 Roll the marble again. When it reaches the floor, try to change its direction by blowing on it. **Record** what happens.

Find Out More!

Experiment with pulls. Use a steel ball and a magnet. How can you change the motion of the ball without touching it?

4 Roll the marble again. This time, try to make it speed up by blowing on it. Then try to make it slow down. **Record** what you do and what happens.

Think! How did you use pushes to change the motion of the marble?

Forces and Motion

Pushes and pulls are **forces**. Forces can change how fast an object is moving. This skater is using forces to speed up and slow down. To speed up, the skater pushes harder with one foot and then with the other. To stop, she drags the brake on the back of her skate. Dragging pulls her to a stop.

Forces can also change the direction in which an object is moving. As the skater rolls along, she pushes against one skate. The pushing makes her turn. She keeps pushing until she changes direction.

Do you play baseball, soccer, or basketball? Then you know about balls in motion. Think about the ball in each sport. How do you use forces to make it move, speed up, slow down, or change direction?

You know how people use forces to move objects.
In what other ways are forces made to move things?

◀ A tractor can pull
heavy farm machinery.

Magnets pull on some metal
objects. The force of a
magnet can move an object
without touching it. ▶

◀ A bulldozer
makes it easier
to push soil
and rocks.

Sometimes it is hard to see where a push or pull is coming from. The earth pulls on everything near it. This pull is called the force of **gravity**.

The force of gravity pulls objects toward the center of the earth. This ballet dancer will come back down to the floor because of gravity.

> **Reading Check** **Draw a picture** of an object in motion. Tell how a force can change the motion.

Word Power

If you need help, turn to the pages shown in blue.

Match a word with a picture. (B10–B11)

transparent   translucent   opaque

1.   **2.**   **3.**

Use these words to fill in the blanks.

light   lens   forces
gravity   reflects

4. A _____ bends light as the light passes through.
(B16–B17)

5. _____ moves in straight lines. (B4–B5)

6. A mirror _____ light. (B6–B7)

7. Pushes and pulls are _____ . (B24–B25)

8. The force of _____ pulls everything toward the
earth. (B26–B27)

Solving Science Problems

You want to cut out shapes to make dark shadows
on the wall. Read the list of materials. Choose the
ones you think will work best. Tell why you chose
each one.

plastic wrap   tissue paper   wood
wax paper   cardboard   paper bag
aluminum foil   paper napkin

People Using Science

Lighting Technician

Lighting technicians use lights on stage for special effects. Red lights can look like fire. Flashing lights can look like lightning. Yellow lights can look like sunshine.

This lighting technician keeps track of which lights to use in each scene of a play. Why is it important to know which lights to use?

 Using Math ## Comparing Numbers

Compare the speeds of the animals in the pictures. Then answer the questions.

cheetah 70mph Kangaroo 30mph elephant 22mph human 20mph jack rabbit 45mph

1. Which animal moves faster than a jack rabbit?

2. Is a human faster or slower than a kangaroo?

3. What might happen if an elephant and a human were in a race?

4. List the animals in order from slowest to fastest.

LESSON 6

What does motion have to do with sound?

Activity
Observing Motion and Sound

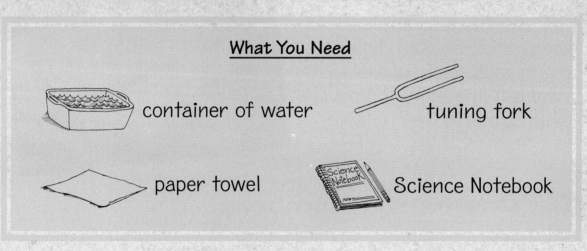

What You Need

container of water

tuning fork

paper towel

Science Notebook

1 Hold a tuning fork near your ear. **Talk about** and **record** what you hear.

2 Strike the tuning fork on the bottom of your shoe. Touch it with one finger. **Talk about** and **record** what you feel.

3 Strike the tuning fork again. Hold it near your ear. **Talk about** and **record** what you hear.

4 Strike the tuning fork again. Lower it slowly into some water. **Record** what you see on the surface of the water.

Think! What caused what you saw on the surface of the water?

Wiggles and Waves

Suppose you put a stick in water. Then you wiggle the stick back and forth quickly. This kind of motion is called a **vibration**.

Look at the picture. The stick makes the water move. **Waves** form and move away from the stick. You can see the waves on the surface of the water.

Waves can move through air, too. Suppose you pluck a harp string. It vibrates back and forth. It makes waves in the air around it. The waves spread out through the air. You cannot see these waves. However, you can hear them. Vibrations that make waves you hear are called **sound**.

> **Reading Check** **Tell** about waves that you can see and waves that you can't see.

How can sounds be different?

Activity

Experimenting With High and Low Sounds

What You Need

 paper cup

 rubber band

 goggles

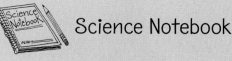 Science Notebook

1 Stretch a rubber band over the opening of a cup.

2 Hold the cup near your ear. Gently pluck the rubber band. Listen to the sound. **Record** what you hear.

3 Squeeze the cup to change the shape of the opening. **Predict** what you will hear. Then repeat step 2.

Think! How did the sounds you made compare?

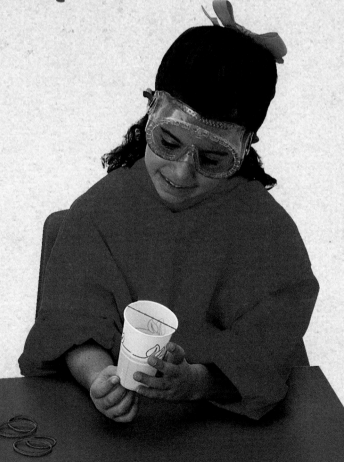

 **Find Out More!**

CD-ROM

Use **Science Blaster Jr.** to find out more about sound. Create and play songs. Listen to them and see how the waves change.

High and Low, Loud and Soft

Vibrations can be slow. Vibrations can be fast. Slow vibrations make a low sound. A gong makes a low sound.

Fast vibrations make a high sound. Finger cymbals vibrate faster than a gong. They make a high sound. **Pitch** is how high or how low a sound is.

Sounds can be soft. Sounds can be loud. The ticking of a clock is a very soft sound. A clock's alarm is a very loud sound.

The loudness of a sound is called its **volume**. Radios and televisions have volume controls. You use these controls to make the sounds that you hear louder or softer. On what other objects might you change the volume of a sound?

These sound makers have been put in order by their volume. The softest sound is a baby breathing. The sound a vacuum cleaner makes is louder than the sound of a ringing telephone. Two girls talking is a softer sound than a rock band playing.

The loudest sound is a jet taking off. Sounds as loud as the engine of a jet can hurt people's ears. That is why the worker is wearing ear protection.

Soft

Using Math

Answer these questions about the order of the pictures. The softest sound is first.

1. Which sound is third?
2. Which sound is fifth?
3. Which sound is second?
4. Is the fourth sound or the sixth sound louder?

Reading Check **Write** about some sound makers you know. Describe the pitch and volume of their sounds.

LESSON 8

How is heat made?

Activity

Exploring Motion and Heat

What You Need

2 pencils   goggles   Science Notebook

1 Hold two pencils to your cheeks. **Observe** how hot or cold they feel.

2 Rub one pencil against the other 20 times.

3 Hold the pencils to your cheeks again. **Observe** and **record** how hot or cold they feel.

4 Hold your hands to your cheeks. **Observe** how hot or cold they feel.

5 **Predict** how your hands will feel when you rub them together 20 times. **Test** it out. **Record** what happens.

Think! What did you do to the pencils and your hands to make heat?

Internet Field Trip

Visit **www.eduplace.com** to find out more about heat.

Making Heat

There are many ways to make heat. How many can you name in the picture?

Objects in motion can make **heat**. That is why people rub their arms with their hands to warm up. Bicycle brakes get hot when they rub against the wheel. Whenever two surfaces rub together, heat is made.

Burning things also make heat. Burning wood in a campfire makes a lot of heat. Burning charcoal in a grill also makes a lot of heat.

Light from the sun makes heat, too. In the picture the sun is making the sand on the beach very hot. What else is being warmed by the sun?

> ✔ **Reading Check** **Draw a picture** of three different ways to make heat.

How can heat be used and saved?

Activity
Exploring Ways to Save Heat

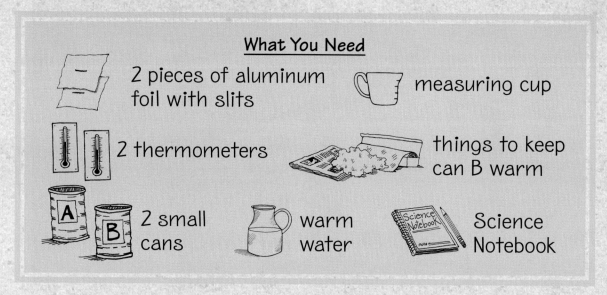

What You Need

2 pieces of aluminum foil with slits

measuring cup

2 thermometers

things to keep can B warm

2 small cans

warm water

Science Notebook

1 **Make a plan** to keep a can of water warm. **Record** your plan.

2 Pour 1 cup of warm water into can A and can B. Cover the cans with foil pieces. Put a thermometer through the slit into the water in each can.

3 Wait 1 minute. **Measure** and **record** the water temperature in each can. Use can B to **test your plan.**

4 Wait 10 minutes. **Measure** and **record** the water temperature in each can.

Find Out More!

How do people use heat? Make a plan to find out. Try out your plan. Report what you find.

Exploring Ways to Save Heat		
	Can A	Can B
Temperature after 1 minute		
Temperature after 10 minutes		

Think! How did your plan keep the water in can B warm?

Using Natural Resources

The earth includes many living and nonliving things. Trees and fish are some living things. Rocks, soil, water, and air are nonliving things. All of these things are used by people. They are **natural resources**.

Some natural resources are used for food. Some are used for shelter. Some are used to make heat.

People use heat to cook food and warm their homes. Gas, oil, coal, and wood are some of the natural resources used to make heat. People can save these natural resources by using only as much as they need. What other natural resources do people use for heat?

Reading Check Write a story about people who use and save heat from natural resources.

Word Power

If you need help, turn to the pages shown in blue.

Match a word with a picture. (B13, B16, B32)

shadow   lens   waves

1.   2.   3.

Write the letter of the correct word.

4. A ball rolling is an object in _____. (B20–B21)
   a. motion   **b.** sound   **c.** pitch   **d.** volume

5. How fast something moves is its _____. (B20–B21)
   a. gravity   **b.** shadow   **c.** speed   **d.** vibration

6. A _____ is a back-and-forth motion. (B32–B33)
   a. light   **b.** volume   **c.** shadow   **d.** vibration

7. The _____ of an instrument is how high or low it sounds. (B36–B37)
   a. wave   **b.** pitch   **c.** volume   **d.** speed

8. The loudness of a sound is its _____. (B36–B37)
   a. wave   **b.** pitch   **c.** volume   **d.** speed

9. Rubbing two objects together will make _____. (B42–B43)
   a. gravity   **b.** sound   **c.** heat   **d.** pitch

10. We use some of the earth's _____ to make heat.
   (B46–B47)
   a. motion   **b.** speed   **c.** gravity   **d.** natural resources

Using Science Ideas

How many examples of motion can you find in this picture? List them.

Writing in Science

Besides being used to make heat, trees have many other uses. Make a list of the ways trees are used. Then list ways to save this natural resource.

Cause and Effect

Look at each picture and read the sentence that tells about it. Write or draw one effect for each action.

▲ Hope rubs her hands together.

▲ Amy pushes hard with her foot.

▲ A mirror is in the path of light.

▲ Sam turns the volume down on the radio.

Use Data From a Picture

Use the picture to answer the questions.

1. Which ball moved the greatest distance?

2. Which ball moved the least distance?

3. How many meters did the red team's balls move altogether?

4. How many meters did the blue team's balls move altogether?

5. How much farther did ball 4 move than ball 2?

UNIT C

Changes Over Time

Themes: Models; Scale; Constancy and Change

1 What was the earth like a long time ago?

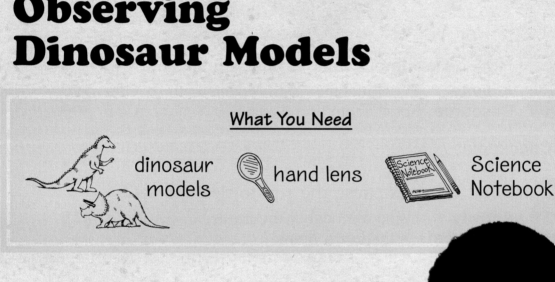

Activity
Observing Dinosaur Models

What You Need

dinosaur models   hand lens   Science Notebook

1 Choose two very different dinosaur models.

2 Use a hand lens to **observe** the models.

③ **Draw** the two dinosaurs you chose.

④ **Talk about** how these dinosaurs were alike and different. **Record** your ideas.

Think! How is a model dinosaur different from a real dinosaur?

Internet Field Trip

Visit **www.eduplace.com** to find out more about different kinds of dinosaurs.

Diplodocus

Ornitholestes

The Time of the Dinosaurs

Millions of years ago, many kinds of **dinosaurs** lived on the earth. All dinosaurs had four limbs and a tail. Yet, they were different in many ways. Brachiosaurus walked on all four legs. Allosaurus walked on two legs. Diplodocus had a very long neck. Ornitholestes had a short neck.

Brachiosaurus

Allosaurus

When dinosaurs were alive, there were many
erupting volcanoes. The weather was hot, year after
year. Then the earth changed. All the kinds of
dinosaurs died. They became **extinct**. There are no
more living dinosaurs. Yet, their body shapes and
parts looked like some kinds of animals alive today.

Reading Check Draw a picture of a dinosaur.
Draw an animal alive today. Show how they are alike.

LESSON 2
How big were the dinosaurs?

Activity
Measuring Dinosaurs

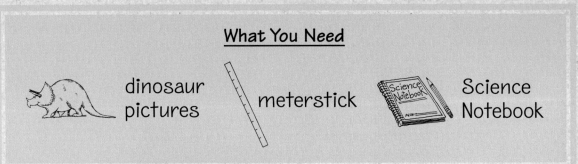

What You Need

dinosaur pictures   meterstick   Science Notebook

1. Stand next to the dinosaur picture on the wall and **compare** the size of the dinosaur to your size.

2 **Measure** the length of the dinosaur. **Record** the length.

3 Repeat steps 1 and 2 for each dinosaur picture.

4 **Make a bar graph** to **compare** the lengths of the three dinosaurs.

Think! Which of these dinosaurs were bigger than you? Which one was smaller?

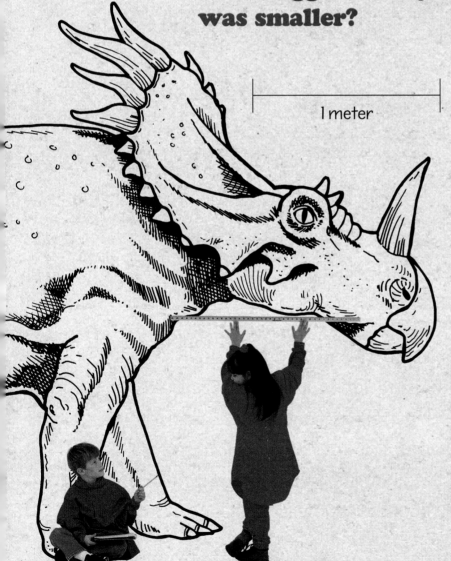

1 meter

Find Out More!

CD-ROM

How big were other kinds of dinosaurs? Use **Science Blaster™ Jr.** to compare Apatosaurus to Triceratops.

Lambeosaurus

Dinosaur Sizes

Dinosaurs were many sizes. This picture compares them to things we know today. Find Lambeosaurus. It was about 15 meters (50 feet) long. That's longer than a boxcar! Now find Triceratops. It was 9 meters (30 feet) long. That's as long as a school bus! Look at the size of Velociraptor. It was only about 2 meters (6 feet) long.

CHANGES OVER TIME

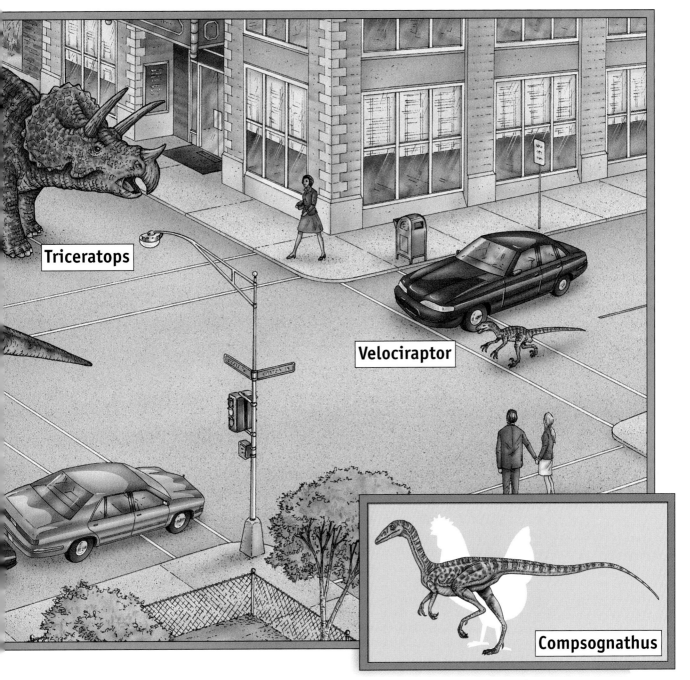

Triceratops

Velociraptor

Compsognathus

Other dinosaurs were bigger and smaller than these. Brachiosaurus was 12 meters (40 feet) tall. Compsognathus was not much bigger than a chicken. It was about 76 centimeters (30 inches) long. Seismosaurus was the longest at 51 meters (170 feet). That's twice as long as a basketball court!

Reading Check About how many Velociraptors long was one Lambeosaurus? **Draw a picture** to show it.

How do we know about animals of long ago?

Activity
Digging for Bones

What You Need

goggles   paintbrush   plastic spoons

container of wet sand   paper plates

newspapers   Science Notebook

① Pretend you are a scientist digging for dinosaur bones. Use a spoon to carefully dig in some sand. Put the sand on a paper plate.

2 Stop digging when you find a bone. Use a paintbrush to gently brush away the rest of the sand.

3 Place any bones you find on another paper plate.

Find Out More!

What else do you want to know about the bone you found? List some questions. Plan how to find the answers. Share your plan.

4 Make a **sketch** of your findings.

Think! What can you learn from the bones you found?

Puzzles From Long Ago

Think about putting together a puzzle. Dinosaur bones are like pieces of a puzzle. Scientists may find some dinosaur bones. They put the bones together to make a **skeleton**. From the skeleton, they learn about a dinosaur's size and shape. They can compare the skeleton to those of other kinds of dinosaurs.

Corythosaurus skeleton

How Do You Know How Old?

Look at the skeleton of Corythosaurus. Its back leg bones are much longer than its front leg bones. What might this mean? It probably walked on two legs. The bones in its tail are very wide. It probably held up its thick tail for balance as it walked. Find the bump on the head of the skeleton. Scientists found that it is hollow. Turn the page to see how this dinosaur might have looked when it was alive.

An artist painted over the photo of the skeleton.
Now the picture shows how a living Corythosaurus
might have looked. The artist chose the skin colors.
Nobody knows for sure what colors dinosaurs were.

The bump on Corythosaurus's head is called a
crest. The crest might have been used to make loud
sounds. It might have been used to scare away other
animals or to find a mate. What do you think?

Corythosaurus

ᴏ You Know How Old?

s and Bones

Corythosaurus was a kind of duck-billed dinosaur. Look at its mouth to see why. Skeletons of whole families of duck-billed dinosaurs have been found together. Nests were found, too. The babies in the nests were very small. Scientists think this shows that duck-billed dinosaurs cared for their young.

Reading Check Pretend you are a scientist. You find some very big bones. **Write** what you could learn.

LESSON 4
How do fossils form over time?

Activity
Exploring Fossils

What You Need

goggles

paper plate

once-living objects

2 fossils

hand lens

dough

Science Notebook

1 Use a hand lens to **observe** two fossils. **Draw** what you see.

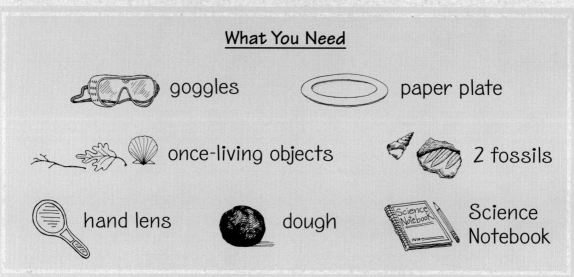

2 **Talk about** what kinds of living things made these fossils. **Decide** if they were plants or animals.

3 **Draw** how you think these plants or animals looked.

4 Flatten some dough on a paper plate. Press an object into the dough and carefully remove it. This is a model fossil.

5 **Compare** the model you made with the real fossils.

Think! Which fossil is more like the model you made? Tell why.

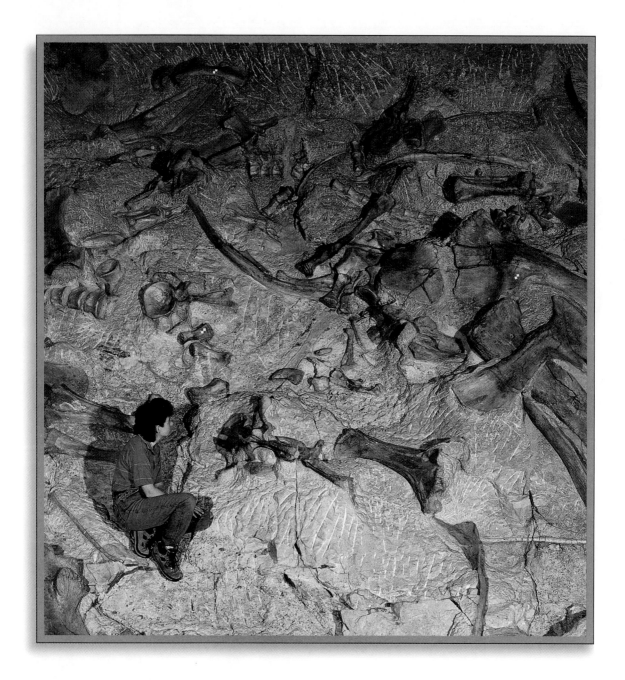

Slow Changes

When some dinosaurs died, mud covered them.
The soft parts of their bodies rotted. Millions of years
passed. Slowly, the hard parts of their bodies changed
into rock. These parts of once-living things are called
fossil remains. Dinosaur bones, shark teeth, snail
shells, and tree trunks may become fossil remains.

The shape of a leaf in rock is also a trace fossil. The leaf rotted but its outline is still there. ▶

Other fossils are a clue, or trace, of what a living thing did or how it looked. Millions of years ago, a dinosaur walked on soft mud. Footprints were left. Slowly, the mud changed into hard rock. Years later, the footprints in rock are found. They are called **trace fossils**. They show how the dinosaur moved.

Reading Check **Write a story** about some trace fossils and fossil remains. Tell how they formed.

How do we know what extinct animals ate?

Activity
Experimenting With Model Teeth

What You Need

2 tree leaves   goggles

dry cereal   2 small blocks of wood

2 golf tees   timer   Science Notebook

1 Pretend that two blocks of wood are flat teeth. Grind a leaf between the blocks for 1 minute. **Record** how the leaf changes.

2 Pretend that two golf tees are pointed teeth. Tear a second leaf with the golf tees for 1 minute. **Record** how the leaf changes.

Experimenting With Model Teeth

Kind of "Food"	Grinding With Blocks	Tearing With Golf Tees
Leaves		

3 Repeat steps 1 and 2, using a few pieces of cereal.

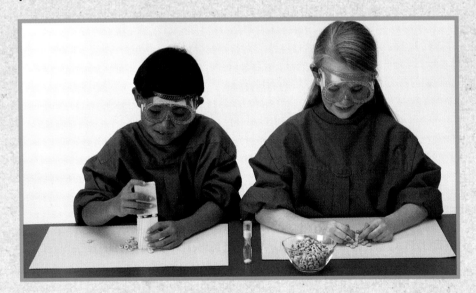

Think! What do flat teeth do better, and what do pointed teeth do better?

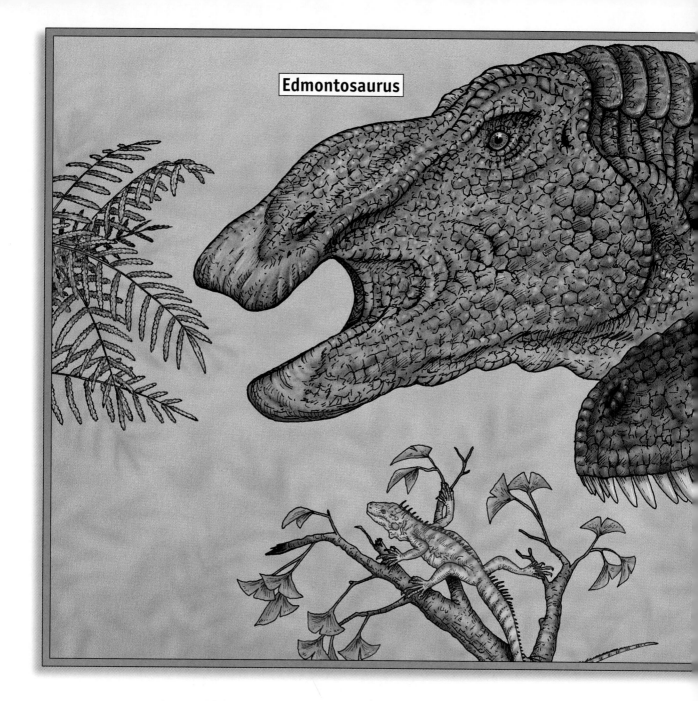
Edmontosaurus

Fossil Teeth and Skulls

Look at the mouths of the two dinosaurs. How are they different? Why can't you see Edmontosaurus's teeth? Edmontosaurus was a duck-billed dinosaur. Its teeth were far back in its mouth.

Which dinosaur do you think ate plants? Which dinosaur do you think ate meat?

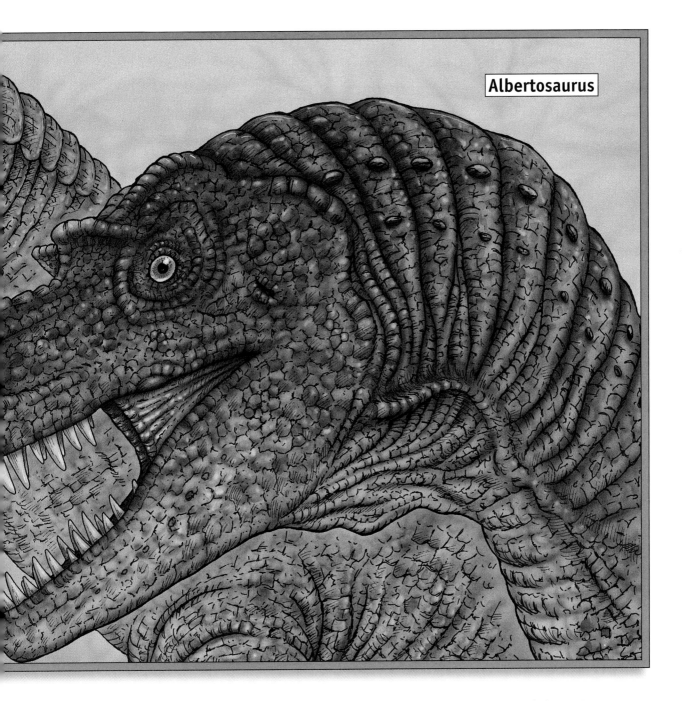

Scientists look at the shape and sharpness of fossil teeth. They compare them to the teeth of animals alive today. They also look at the shape of the mouth. Then they can guess what foods some dinosaurs ate.

Most plant-eating dinosaurs had **flat teeth** to grind plants. Most meat eaters had sharp, **pointed teeth** to tear meat. Turn the page to see inside the mouths of dinosaurs in the picture.

Edmontosaurus

This picture shows the teeth and skulls of the dinosaurs. A **skull** is the part of the skeleton inside the head. Edmontosaurus had blunt, flat teeth far back in its mouth. It was a plant eater. The front of its mouth was a hard beak, like a duck's bill.

Albertosaurus had pointed teeth near the front of its mouth. It did not have back teeth. This dinosaur tore off pieces of meat that were small enough to swallow.

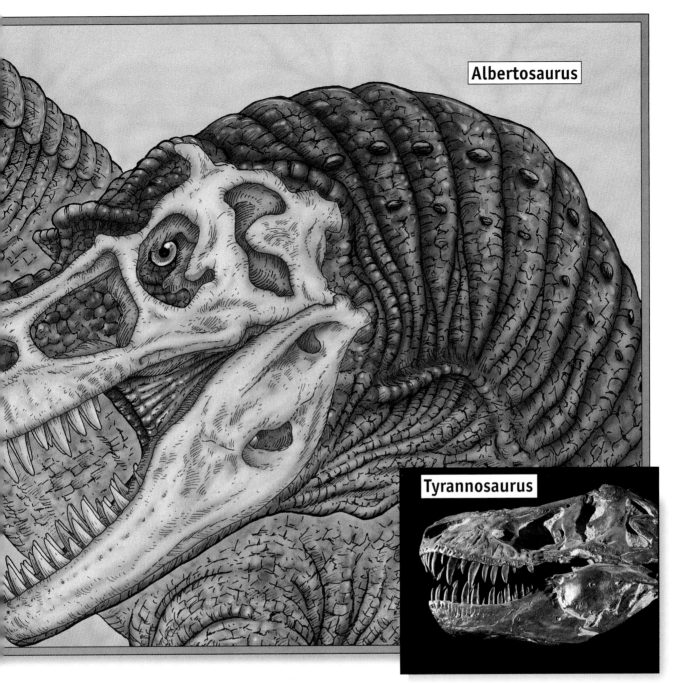

Albertosaurus

Tyrannosaurus

Tyrannosaurus's skull was almost one and a half meters (about 4 feet) long. It had teeth that were 15 centimeters (6 inches) long. They were pointed like knives. Each tooth had edges like a saw. What do you think it ate? Tyrannosaurus was a meat eater. In fact, it may have hunted big duck-billed dinosaurs.

Reading Check Suppose you found a dinosaur skull. **Tell** how you would decide what it ate.

Word Power

If you need help, turn to the pages shown in blue.

Match the words with a picture. (C18–C19)

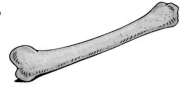

1.  **2.**

Use these words to fill in the blanks.

extinct   skeleton
dinosaur   skull

3. All the bones in an animal's body are its _____.
(C12–C13)

4. The part of the skeleton inside the head is
the _____. (C24–C25)

5. When all the living things of one kind die, they
become _____. (C4–C5)

6. A _____ is an animal that lived on the earth
millions of years ago. (C4–C5)

Solving Science Problems

You are a fossil hunter. You must choose fossil-digging
tools to carry in your backpack. Decide which tools you
would take. Explain your choices.

hammer   snow shovel   toothbrush
broom   screwdriver   vacuum cleaner

People Using Science

Paleontologist

Paleontologists are scientists who study fossils. They may go on trips to search for fossils. When they find some, they may dig them up.

The fossils are taken to a museum. There the paleontologist sorts and identifies them.

Look at the picture. Why do you think the fossils are wrapped so carefully?

Using Math Finding a Pattern

Kate went on a dinosaur dig. On Monday she found 4 Edmontosaurus teeth. On Tuesday she found 7 Edmontosaurus teeth. On Wednesday she found 10.

Monday

Tuesday

Wednesday

Use the data above to answer each question.

1. What is the pattern?
2. If the pattern continues, how many teeth will Kate find on Thursday?
3. How many will she find on Saturday?

What changes cause the sun to rise and set?

Activity

Using a Model of the Earth

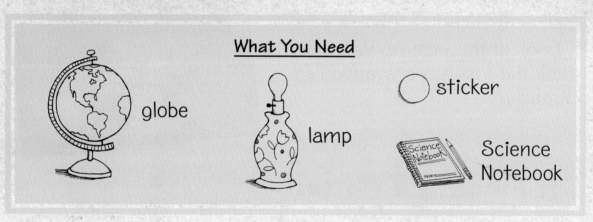

What You Need

globe

lamp

sticker

Science Notebook

1. Put a globe in the middle of the room. Find the place on the globe where you live. Use a sticker to mark your place.

2 Darken the room. Turn on a lamp in the corner of the room. The lamp is a model of the sun.

3 Turn the globe slowly in place. **Observe** when the sticker is in the dark and in the light. **Record** what you see.

Think! **What part of the day is it when your place on the earth is starting to face the sun? Tell why.**

Internet Field Trip

Visit **www.eduplace.com** to learn more about sunrises and sunsets.

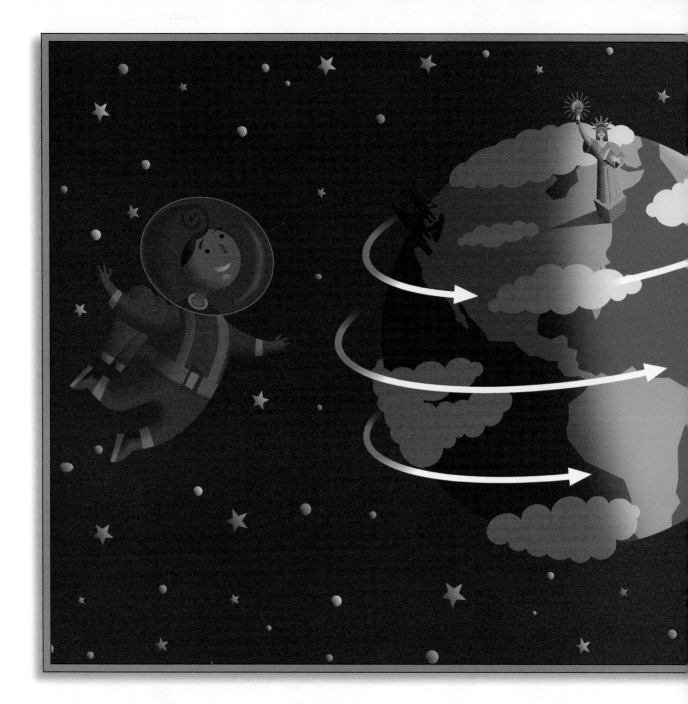

As the Earth Spins

Some changes on the earth take millions of years.
Others take only a day. Each morning the sun seems
to rise in the east and follow a path across the sky.
In the evening the sun disappears in the west.
People used to think the sun moved in a circle
around the earth.

If you could look at the earth from space, you would see something different. The sun seems to stay in one place, and the earth turns, or **rotates**. It takes 24 hours to make one turn. As your part of the earth turns to face the sun, it is **sunrise**. As your part of the earth turns away from the sun, it is **sunset**.

Reading Check Pretend you are the earth and a partner is the sun. **Act out** what makes sunrise and sunset.

How does the night sky change?

Activity

Making a Model of Moon Phases

What You Need

lamp

goggles

foam ball

pencil

Science Notebook

❶ Use a foam ball as a **model** of the moon. Carefully push a pencil into the ball.

❷ Darken the room. Turn on a lamp in the room. The lamp is a model of the sun.

3 Stand or sit where you can see the "sun." You are the model of the earth.

4 Have a partner move the "moon" slowly around you. **Observe** changes in the amount of "sunlight" on the "moon."

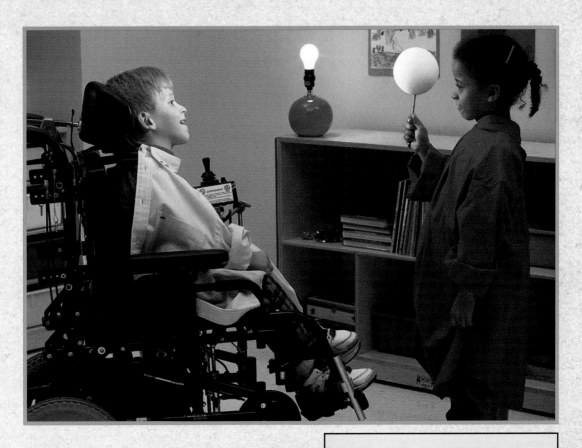

5 **Record** some of the shapes you observed.

Think! What makes the moon seem to change shape?

Find Out More!

Look outside at night to find the moon. Record where in the sky it is. Predict where it will be in one hour. Check your prediction. Measure and record how much the moon's position changed.

Changes in the Night Sky

The moon does not give off its own light. The moon **reflects** sunlight. That means sunlight hits the moon and bounces off it. The side of the moon that is facing the sun is lighted. The other side of the moon is dark. Most nights you see only part of the lighted side.

Phases of the Moon

Day 1

Day 28

Day 4

Day 22

Day 8

Day 18

Day 12

Day 15

How the moon looks from the earth changes from night to night. One night the lighted part that you see looks like a backward C. After many nights it looks like a circle. On that night there is a full moon. In the nights after the full moon, the lighted part you see gets smaller. These changes are called the **phases** of the moon. The pattern of phases takes about 28 days.

Midnight

8:00 P.M.

You can also see changes in the sky in just one night. If you check the moon every hour, you will see it seem to rise, move across the sky, and set just like the sun. The sun and moon both seem to move because the earth rotates.

Pretend you are camping outdoors. You lie back in your sleeping bag. Imagine what the stars in the sky would look like.

CHANGES OVER TIME

4:00 A.M.

Most stars also seem to move during the night. You may know the outlined group of stars in the pictures as the Big Dipper. In just a few hours you can watch the Big Dipper turn in the sky. Like the moon and sun, stars also seem to move. This is because the earth rotates.

Reading Check **Draw two pictures**. Show how the night sky changes.

Activity
Measuring Air Temperature

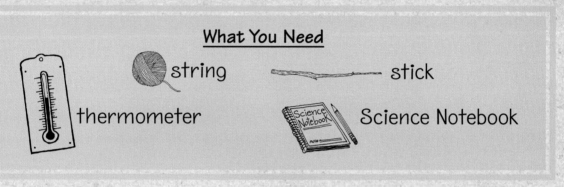

What You Need

string

stick

thermometer

Science Notebook

1 Tie one end of a piece of string to a thermometer. Tie the other end of the string to a stick.

2 Find a spot outdoors that is shady all day. **Plan** two times to **measure** the air temperature in that spot. Choose an early-morning time and an afternoon time.

3 Go to the shady spot at the times you chose. Hold the thermometer away from the ground and walls.

4 Wait 1 minute. Read and **record** the air temperature.

Measuring Air Temperature					
	Day 1	Day 2	Day 3	Day 4	Day 5
Morning temperature					
Afternoon temperature					

5 Repeat steps 3 and 4 for four more days.

Think! What temperature pattern did you see each day?

Weather Patterns

You know that the weather changes from day to day. One day can be sunny and the next can be cloudy. Weather also changes from hour to hour. Look at the three pictures of the same city. The pictures were taken at three different times during a day. How do you think the weather changed?

You can see how the sky changed from hour to hour. In the morning the sky over the city was clear and blue. Later in the morning white puffy clouds appeared. In the afternoon the clouds became gray and covered the sky. Then there was a thunderstorm.

The changes in the sky and clouds form a pattern. Some places in the world have a weather pattern like this day after day in the summer.

Changes in air temperature also form a weather pattern. Follow these children during a single day. What changes do you see?

8:00 A.M.

In the morning the air temperature is low.

Noon

During the day the temperature rises.

Lemonade

4:00 P.M.

In the late afternoon the temperature is high.

4

11:00 P.M.

During the night the temperature falls.

Using Math Copy the chart below. Write the time shown in each picture. Write the temperature shown on each thermometer.

	Picture 1	Picture 2	Picture 3	Picture 4
Time	___:___	___:___	___:___	___:___
Temperature	___°F	___°F	___°F	___°F

1. At what time was the temperature the highest?

2. At what time was it the lowest?

Reading Check Tell how the air temperature changes during a day.

How does the weather change over the seasons?

Activity
Comparing Seasons

What You Need

 crayons

 Science Notebook

1 Go outdoors. **Observe** the trees and other plants. **Observe** what animals are doing. Notice the clothes people wear.

2 **Draw a picture** of the season you observed. Show what the weather is like in this season. Name the season.

3 **Draw a picture** for each of the other seasons of the year. Show how some things change color from season to season.

Think! How does the weather change from season to season?

Find Out More!

Measure the air temperature and rainfall from one season to the next. Compare the data for two seasons. Tell how they are different.

Changing Seasons

Look at the pictures above. They show the same place in winter and summer. In winter the weather is cold and snowy here. In spring the air slowly warms. By summer it is hot. Even the rain feels warm. In the autumn the air slowly cools. If you live where the map is colored pink, then your seasons are similar.

The pictures on this page show winter and summer in part of California. In this part of California the air temperature is warm in every season. In winter the weather is very rainy. The rain helps the grass grow and stay green. In summer it almost never rains. The grass stops growing and turns brown.

> ✔ **Reading Check** **Write** about what you do in each season. Tell how the weather changes where you live.

Word Power

If you need help, turn to the pages shown in blue.

Match a word with a picture. (C4, C12, C24)

skull   dinosaur   skeleton

1.   **2.**   **3.**

Write the letter of the correct words.

4. As the earth _____ we see sunrise and sunset. (C30–C31)

a. rises   **b.** sets   **c.** rotates   **d.** holds still

5. Changes in the way the moon looks are _____. (C34–C35)

a. seasons   **b.** phases   **c.** weather   **d.** sunset

6. The moon _____ the light of the sun. (C34–C35)

a. makes   **b.** rises   **c.** sets   **d.** reflects

7. Some dinosaurs used _____ to grind plants. (C22–C23)

a. flat teeth   **b.** skeletons   **c.** skulls   **d.** pointed teeth

8. Some dinosaurs used _____ to tear meat. (C22–C23)

a. skeletons   **b.** flat teeth   **c.** skulls   **d.** pointed teeth

9. As your part of the earth turns to face the sun, it is _____.
(C30–C31)

a. phases   **b.** rotates   **c.** sunrise   **d.** sunset

10. As your part of the earth turns away from the sun, it is
_____. (C30–C31)

a. phases   **b.** rotates   **c.** sunrise   **d.** sunset

Using Science Ideas

What two things can you tell about this dinosaur by looking at its skeleton?

Writing in Science

Your aunt has promised to do some activities with you. Look at the list of activities.

go ice-skating	go boating	fly a kite
go to a movie	go swimming	go to a museum

Decide what kind of weather would be best for each activity. Decide which season would be best for each activity. Explain how you made your decisions. Then write a letter to your aunt. Tell about one thing you would like to do and why.

Using Reading Skills

Sequence

Sara looked for the moon each night. She drew it every time she could see it. On a sheet of paper, draw how the moon looked on the days Sara missed.

Look at the pattern of moon shapes on the calendar. What do you think the pattern would be for the next month?

Crayons

February

Sunday	Monday	Tuesday	Wednesday	Thursday	Friday	Saturday
1	2	3	4	5	6	7
8	9	10	11	12	13	14
15	16	17	18	19	20	21
22	23	24	25	26	27	28

Using MATH SKILLS

Using a Table

The Clark family plans to visit the Grand Canyon. They want to pick a month with good weather. The table shows high and low temperatures for five months.

Grand Canyon		
Month	High Temperature	Low Temperature
May	70°F	39°F
June	81°F	47°F
July	84°F	54°F
August	82°F	53°F
September	76°F	47°F

Use the table to answer each question.

1. In which month are temperatures the highest?

2. In which month are temperatures the lowest?

3. The Clarks want to go in July. What is the difference between the high and low temperatures in that month?

4. Will temperatures in October be higher or lower than in September? How do you know?

Solids, Liquids, and Gases

Theme: Constancy and Change

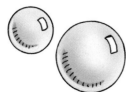

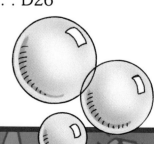

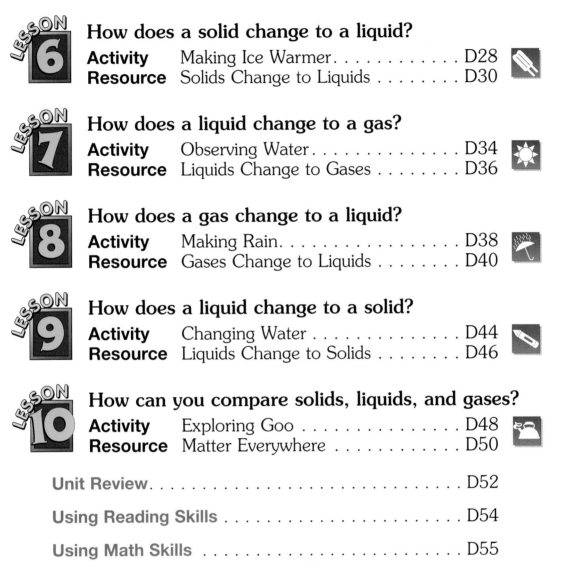

How can you describe and group solids?

Activity

Describing and Grouping Solids

What You Need

piece of plastic   counter

marble   paper clip   ball

button   lid   piece of metal

piece of wood   Science Notebook

1 **Observe** and touch some solid objects.

2 Using Math **Group** the objects that are alike in some way.

3 **Draw** and name each group of objects.

4 **Group** the objects in a different way. **Draw** and name each group.

Think! What makes an object a solid?

About Solids

How are the objects in the picture alike? They are made of **matter**. They are solids. A **solid** does not change shape or size when it is moved.

You can describe a solid by its color, shape, size, and texture. The plate is blue and round. It is larger than the cup but smaller than the hat.

SOLIDS, LIQUIDS, AND GASES

The **texture** of an object is how it feels when you touch it. The plate feels smooth.

You can use color, shape, size, or texture to group solids. The plate, the cup, and the coffeepot are all blue objects. The log and the rope have rough textures. Which would you group together by shape? Which would you group by size?

Look at the pictures. Describe some of the solids. Some solids are as soft as a pillow or as hard as a brick. Solids can be smaller than a tiny seed or larger than a tall building. Solids can have a texture as smooth as an apple or as rough as a sidewalk.

Solids can be any color or shape. A pumpkin is a solid. It is hollow with seeds inside, but it does not change its shape when it is moved.

Using
Math

Make a chart like the one below. In each column add objects that are most like the shape shown. Use the pictures to help you.

Space Shapes			
Rectangular Prism	Cube	Cylinder	Sphere
brick			

✔ Reading Check Choose two solid objects. **Write** about how they are alike and how they are different.

How can you describe and group liquids?

Activity

Describing and Grouping Liquids

What You Need

goggles

 cup of orange juice

 cup of colored water

 cup of water

cup of corn syrup

 cup of vegetable oil

 cup of cola

 cup of seltzer water

 paper towels

Science Notebook

 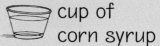 

1 **Look at** some different liquids and **talk about** the color.

2 Gently touch each liquid with your fingers and **talk about** the texture.

3 Think of different ways to group the liquids. **Make a tally chart** to record your groupings.

Using Math

Grouping Liquids		
Group	**Tally**	**Total**

Think! What makes something a liquid?

About Liquids

Do you like to drink liquids? A **liquid** is matter that changes shape when it is moved to another container. Each liquid takes the shape of the glass it is in. If you pour a liquid from a tall glass into one that is short and wide, the liquid will take the shape of the short glass. The liquid still takes up the same amount of space.

How can you describe a liquid? One way is by its color. Milk and grape juice are liquids of different colors. Milk is white. Grape juice is purple. What are the colors of some other liquids?

A liquid can also be described by its texture. Cooking oil feels slippery. Other liquids feel smooth or sticky. What liquids have felt sticky to you?

Find the liquids in these pictures. How can you describe them? Syrup and honey are thick liquids. Thick liquids pour more slowly than thin liquids. Like all liquids, their shapes change when they are poured.

SOLIDS, LIQUIDS, AND GASES

Glue and paint are liquids before they dry. Glue is thick and sticky. Paint can be thick or thin.

What happens to paint and glue after they dry? They no longer change their shapes when they are moved. They have become solids.

> **Reading Check** **Tell** how cooking oil and grape juice are alike and different.

LESSON 3

How are the shapes of solids and liquids different?

Activity
Looking at Shapes

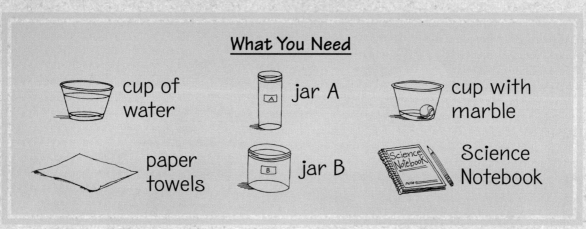

What You Need

- cup of water
- jar A
- cup with marble
- paper towels
- jar B
- Science Notebook

1 Pour water into jar A and **record** its shape.

2 Pour the water from jar A into jar B and **record** its shape.

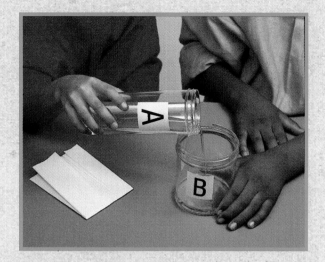

3 Then pour the water back into the cup.

4 Put a marble into jar A and then jar B. **Record** the marble's shape each time.

Think! How are the shapes of the water and the marble different?

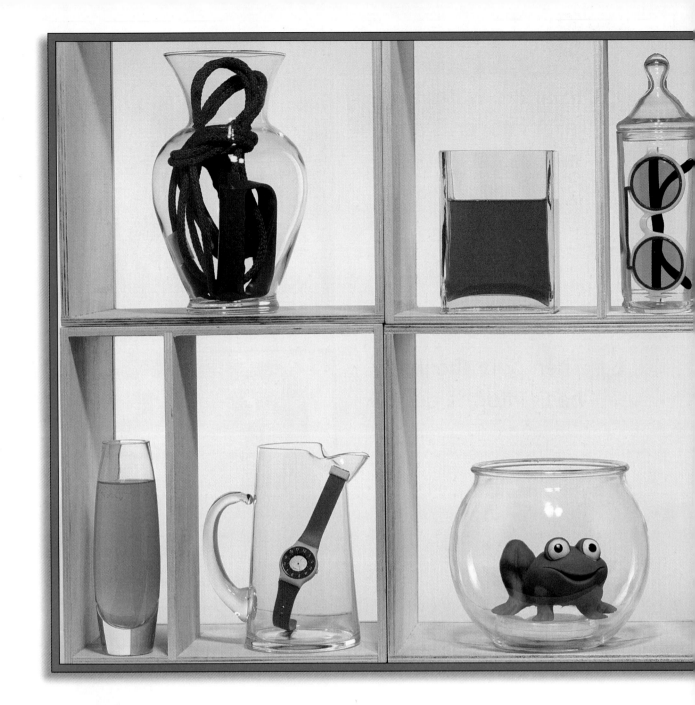

Solid or Liquid

You know that a solid has a definite shape. You also know that a liquid does not. A liquid takes the shape of the container it is in. You can use what you know to tell if something is a solid or a liquid.

Look at the picture. What is in each container? Does each container have a solid or a liquid in it?

The flashlight is a solid because it has a definite shape. It does not take the shape of its container.

Does the pitcher with blue matter in it hold a solid or a liquid? It holds a liquid. You can tell because the matter takes the shape of the container it is in.

> **Reading Check** **Draw** two glass containers. Show a liquid in one container and a solid object in the other.

LESSON 4
How can you describe a gas?

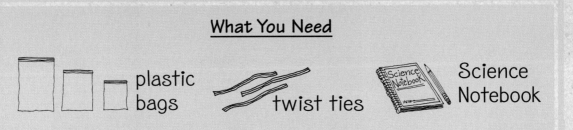

Activity
Trapping Air

What You Need

plastic bags

twist ties

Science Notebook

1 Swish an open bag through the air to fill it. Close it quickly and tie it with a twist tie.

2 **Observe** the air inside the bag. **Record** how it looks.

3 Open the bag and smell the air. **Record** its smell.

4 **Record** the shape and color of the air as you let it out of the bag.

5 Repeat steps 1–4 with other bags.

Think! What makes air a gas?

Internet Field Trip

Visit **www.eduplace.com** to learn more about air.

About Gases

Gas is matter that is all around you and fills many kinds of things. Look at the pictures. There are gases in the balloons, the bubbles, and the ball. A gas fills the walls and floor of the fun house.

Air is a gas that is all around the children. Air is all around you right now. You cannot see air.

A gas does not have a set shape. A gas fills a container and takes its shape. A gas can also change the shape of some containers. As gas is added to a balloon, the balloon changes shape. Not all containers change shape when a gas is added. When air is blown into a glass jar, the jar does not change shape.

Reading Check **Tell** why putting air into a balloon is different from putting air into a bottle.

LESSON 5

How are solids, liquids, and gases alike?

Activity
Looking at Space

What You Need

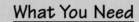

plastic bottle 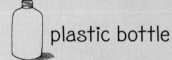 marble 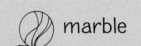 cup of water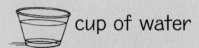

container with water Science Notebook

1 Hold a bottle with the opening toward your partner's arm. Squeeze the bottle and **record** what happens.

2 Quickly push the bottle under the surface of the water in a container. **Record** what happens.

3 Put a marble into a cup of water. **Record** what happens.

Think! What happens when you try to put two kinds of matter into the same space?

Taking Up Space

Look at this picture. The chair, the ball, the toys, the drink container, and the sand are all solids. The juice inside the container and the ocean are liquids.

You cannot see the gases in the picture. The ball is filled with gas. The air, which is all around everything in the picture, is a mixture of gases.

All objects—solids, liquids, and gases—are made of matter. All matter takes up space. Which object in the picture takes up the most space? Do you think it's the ocean, the air, or the beach?

Now think about which object takes up the least space. Maybe it's one tiny grain of sand.

> ✅ **Reading Check** **Act out** what happens when you try to put two kinds of matter in the same space.

Word Power

If you need help, turn to the pages shown in blue.

Match a word with a picture. (D4, D10, D20)

     solid   liquid   gas

1.    **2.**    **3.**

Use these words to fill in the blanks.

    matter   liquid   texture   solid

4. How something feels is its _____. (D4–D5)

5. A _____ does not change shape or size when it is moved. (D4–D5)

6. All objects are made of _____. (D4–D5)

7. A _____ changes shape when it is moved to another container. (D10–D11)

Solving Science Problems

You are a scientist who has just discovered a new kind of matter. You want to describe it to other scientists.

Write about what it looks like. Is it a solid, a liquid, or a gas? Explain how you decided. Then draw a picture of the new matter.

People Using Science

Scuba Diver

A scuba diver uses tanks to carry air underwater. The air in the tanks is a gas for the diver to breathe. When the diver breathes out, bubbles of used air rise in the water.

Some scuba divers study ocean life. Some search for lost things. Other scuba divers study shipwrecks.

Why does the diver need a tank of air underwater?

Making a Tally Chart

Make a tally chart like the one shown. Count the number of solids, liquids, and gases in the picture. Then complete the chart.

Kinds of Matter		
Matter	**Tally**	**Total**
Solid		
Liquid		
Gas		

Use the chart to answer the questions.

1. What is the total number of gases?
2. How many more solids than liquids are there?

LESSON 6

How does a solid change to a liquid?

Activity

Making Ice Warmer

What You Need

 cup with ice cubes

 Science Notebook

1 **Observe** some ice cubes. **Talk about** their size, shape, color, and texture.

2 **Decide** whether ice cubes are a solid, a liquid, or a gas. **Tell** why you think so.

3 **Think of a plan** to make ice cubes warmer. **Record** your plan.

4 **Predict** how the ice cubes will change. **Record** your prediction and test it.

Think! How did the ice cubes change their size, shape, color, and texture?

Find Out More!

CD-ROM

Use **Science Blaster Jr.** Visit the Engineering Room. Model water changing from a solid to a liquid. Then model it changing back to a solid.

Solids Change to Liquids

Are these objects solids, liquids, or gases? They are
solids. Think of ways you can describe their color,
shape, size, and texture. There are yellow bananas,
lemons, and ice pops. The blueberries, oranges, and
limes are round. The raspberries and blueberries are
small. The ice pops and bananas are smooth.

What are the ice pops made of? You probably know they are made of ice. Ice is the solid form of water. Think of what you know about ice. What can happen to ice on a lake when the sun heats it?

Heat can make solid matter change form. What will happen to the solid ice pops if heat is added to them? Turn the page to find out.

How have the ice pops changed? The air around the ice pops was warm. The heat from the warm air made the solid ice pops change form, or **melt**.

Parts of some ice pops are not yet melted. What will happen if the ice pops stay in the warm air? All of the ice pops will probably melt. The heat from the warm air will change them from a solid to a liquid.

SOLIDS, LIQUIDS, AND GASES

The melting ice pops are taking the shape of their plates. How is this a clue that the solid ice pops are changing to a liquid?

You know that ice is the solid form of water. When ice is heated, it changes to liquid water. Where should you keep an ice pop if you do not want it to melt?

> **Reading Check Write** about how a solid can be changed into a liquid.

LESSON 7

How does a liquid change to a gas?

Activity
Observing Water

What You Need

container of water

grease pencil

2 cups

tape

measuring cup

plastic wrap

Science Notebook

1 Put the same amount of water in two cups.

Using Math

2 Mark the water levels with a grease pencil.

3 Cover one cup with a piece of plastic wrap. Put both cups in a sunny place.

4 Wait one day. Look at the cups. **Record** what you see.

Think! How has the water in each cup changed?

Find Out More!

How will the water change over a week? Plan how to measure the changes. Record the data in a bar graph. Use the pattern you see to predict what will happen the next week.

Liquids Change to Gases

Cooling off in water can be fun. The children in the picture are spraying each other with water from a hose. What are some other ways you use water?

What can these children do to get dry if they do not have a towel? They can dry in the sun. They can run around and let the air dry them.

The liquid water on the children's skin changes from a liquid to a gas. The gas is **water vapor**. You cannot see water vapor.

A liquid **evaporates** when it changes to a gas. How do you feel when water evaporates from your skin? You usually feel cooler and drier.

Reading Check Tell about different ways wet clothes can become dry.

LESSON 8
How does a gas change to a liquid?

Activity
Making Rain

What You Need

jar of very warm water

newspapers

pie pan with ice

Science Notebook

1. Feel a pie pan with ice in it. Then feel a jar with warm water in it. **Talk about** how each feels.

2. Carefully place the pie pan on top of the jar of water.

3. **Predict** what you think will happen inside the jar. **Record** your prediction.

4 Watch the jar. Record what happens.

Making Rain
Our prediction
What happened

Think! How did the water in the jar change?

Gases Change to Liquids

You know that there is air all around. Air is a gas that you can't see. Water vapor is another gas. You can't see it. There is water vapor in the air.

Where does the water vapor come from? Water vapor forms when water evaporates. Look at the picture. Where might water vapor come from?

SOLIDS, LIQUIDS, AND GASES

Water from the river warms. It evaporates, or changes to water vapor. The water vapor rises into the air. As it rises, the water vapor in air becomes cooler and cooler.

When water vapor becomes cool enough, it changes to liquid water. A gas **condenses** when it changes to a liquid.

As water vapor rises, it cools. It condenses into tiny water drops that form clouds.

Water from the river evaporates. It changes to water vapor which rises into the air.

Water evaporates from the river. It condenses and forms clouds. The water in clouds falls back to the earth. Some of the water evaporates again. These changes in water make up the **water cycle**.

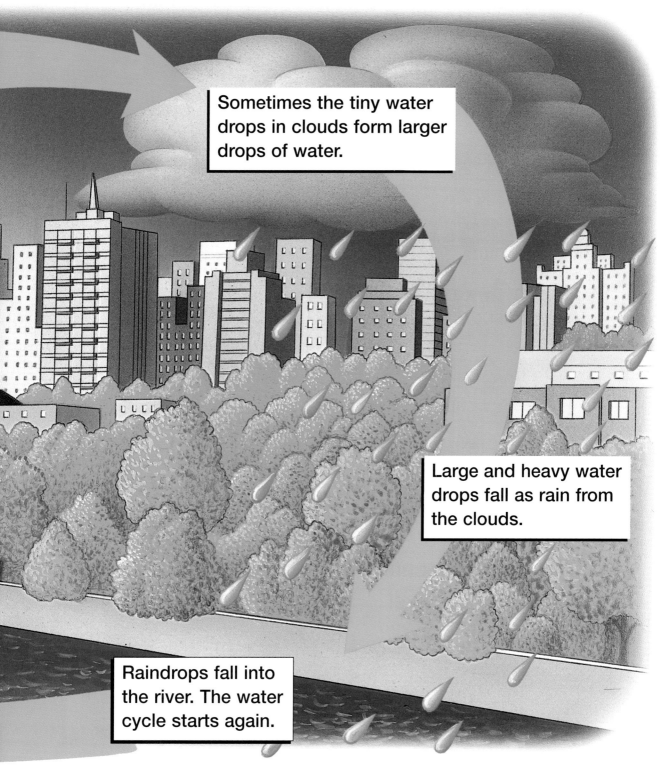

Sometimes the tiny water drops in clouds form larger drops of water.

Large and heavy water drops fall as rain from the clouds.

Raindrops fall into the river. The water cycle starts again.

Find the arrows that point up from the river. They are wavy. These arrows show water evaporating from the river. Follow the arrows through the water cycle.

Reading Check Draw a picture to show the water cycle in another place. Tell about your picture.

How does a liquid change to a solid?

Activity
Changing Water

What You Need

cup   grease pencil

container of water   Science Notebook

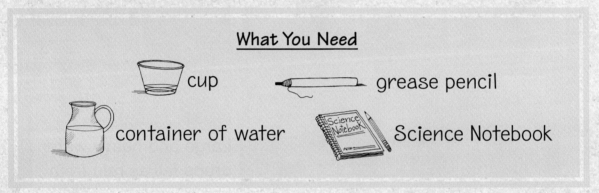

1 Put water into a cup. Mark the water level with a grease pencil.

2 Place the cup of water in a freezer overnight. **Predict** what will happen.

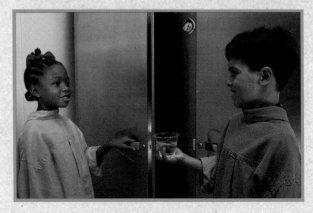

3 **Observe** the cup the next morning. **Record** what you see.

4 **Observe** the cup during the day. **Look at** the level of the water. **Record** what you see.

Find Out More!

What else do you want to know about how things change when they are cooled, heated, or mixed? Ask questions. Make a plan to find answers. Tell about your findings.

Think! What do you notice about the amount of water in the cup?

Making Crayons

▲ melting wax

▲ mixing color

Liquids Change to Solids

Many things were once a different kind of matter than they are now. The pictures show the steps in making crayons. Look at the first picture. It shows liquid wax. Wax is heated to make it melt.

Now look at the second picture. It shows color being mixed into the liquid wax.

▲ sorting crayons

▲ shaping crayons

Crayons

Look at the last two pictures. The liquid wax is poured into molds shaped like crayons. As it cools, the liquid changes to a solid.

A liquid **freezes** when it changes to a solid. Juice can become an ice pop when it cools enough to freeze. What other liquids freeze into useful solids?

> **Reading Check Write** about how you can change a liquid to a solid.

LESSON 10 How can you compare solids, liquids, and gases?

Activity
Exploring Goo

What You Need

 goggles    cup of goo   plastic jar

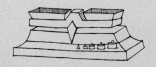 balance   Science Notebook

1 *Using Math* **Observe**, touch, smell, and measure the mass of some goo. Try to pour it into a jar.

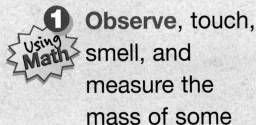

2 **Decide** if the goo is a solid, a liquid, or a gas. **Record** what you think it is and why you think so.

3 **Make a plan** for changing the goo. **Record** your plan.

4 **Predict** and **record** what you think will happen.

5 Carry out your plan and **compare** your findings to your prediction.

Think! How did the goo change? Why?

Internet Field Trip

Visit **www.eduplace.com** to see some solids, liquids, and gases.

Matter Everywhere

Matter is all around you. A solid has a definite size. It also has a definite shape. A liquid has a definite amount. It does not have a definite shape. Gases have no definite size or shape.

Find solids, liquids, and gases in the picture. The next page gives you some examples.

Solids The buildings, the plants, the signs, the stove, and the bathtub are some of the solids.

Liquids The milk in the baby's bottle and the water drops that make up the clouds are some of the liquids.

Gases The balloons, the blimp, the bubbles, and the ball have gases in them.

> **Reading Check Draw a picture** that shows examples of three different kinds of matter.

UNIT D

Word Power

If you need help, turn to the pages shown in blue.

Match a word with a picture. (D4, D10, D20)

solid   liquid   gas

1. 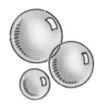   2.    3.

Write the letter of the correct word.

4. When a liquid changes to a solid, it _____. (D46–D47)
   a. melts   **b.** freezes   **c.** evaporates   **d.** condenses

5. When a liquid changes to a gas, it _____. (D36–D37)
   a. melts   **b.** freezes   **c.** evaporates   **d.** condenses

6. When a gas changes to a liquid, it _____. (D40–D41)
   a. melts   **b.** freezes   **c.** evaporates   **d.** condenses

7. When a solid changes to a liquid, it _____. (D32–D33)
   a. melts   **b.** freezes   **c.** evaporates   **d.** condenses

8. When water is a gas, it is called _____. (D36–D37)
   a. matter   **b.** air   **c.** water vapor   **d.** heat

9. _____ can make a solid change form. (D30–D31)
   a. Matter   **b.** Air   **c.** Heat   **d.** Ice

10. Changes that happen to water as it goes into the air and back to earth make up the _____. (D42–D43)
    a. matter   **b.** air   **c.** heat   **d.** water cycle

Using Science Ideas

How many solids, liquids, and gases can you find in the picture? List them.

Writing in Science

Make a chart like the one shown. Add more objects to your chart. Put checks in the right places. Then decide if each thing is a solid, liquid, or gas. Explain each choice in a sentence.

Object	Has its own shape	Takes the shape of its container	Spreads out to fill its container	Kind of matter
rock	✔			solid

Classify

Make a chart like the one below. Fill in the names of solids, liquids, and gases that you see in the picture.

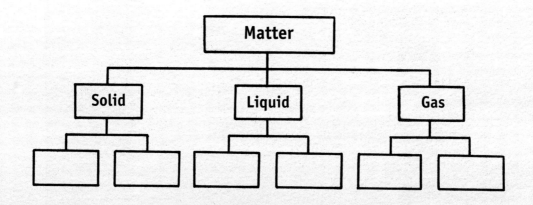

Make a Bar Graph

Fruit Punch

Fruit Punch
6 cups of orange juice
3 cups of pineapple juice
3 cups of grape juice
4 cups of lemonade

Jim made fruit punch for a party. He used this recipe.

Make a bar graph like the one shown below. Color one box for each cup of liquid Jim used.

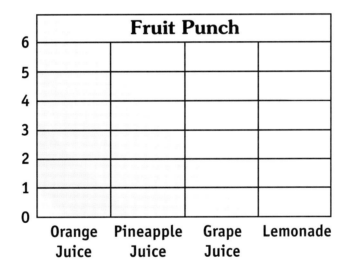

Fruit Punch

	Orange Juice	Pineapple Juice	Grape Juice	Lemonade

(y-axis: 0, 1, 2, 3, 4, 5, 6)

Use the graph to answer each question.

1. Which liquid did Jim use the most?

2. How many more cups of lemonade are in the punch than grape juice?

3. How many fewer cups of pineapple juice are in the punch than orange juice?

4. What is the total number of cups of liquid in the punch?

UNIT E

What Makes Me Sick

Themes: Systems; Scale

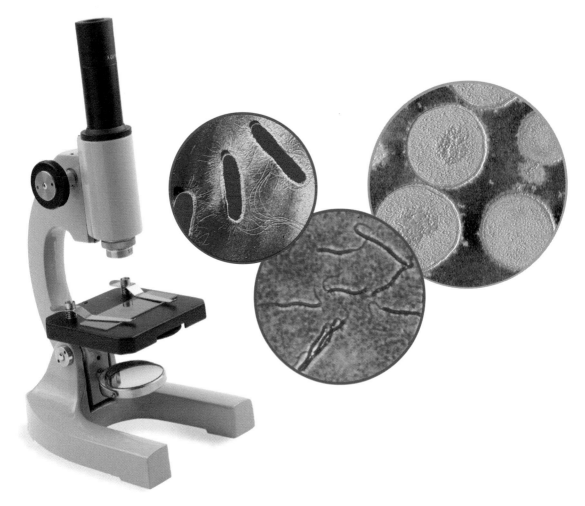

What are germs?

Activity
Making Clay Models

What You Need

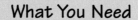

clay paper plate

 pictures of germs Science Notebook

1 Study some microscope pictures of germs. **Look at** the shapes of the germs.

2 Use small pieces of clay to **make models** of the different germs you see.

3 **Draw** your models.

Find Out More!

CD-ROM

Visit the **Science Blaster™ Jr.** time line. Find out when the microscope was invented.

Think! How are your models like real germs? How are they different?

Bacteria

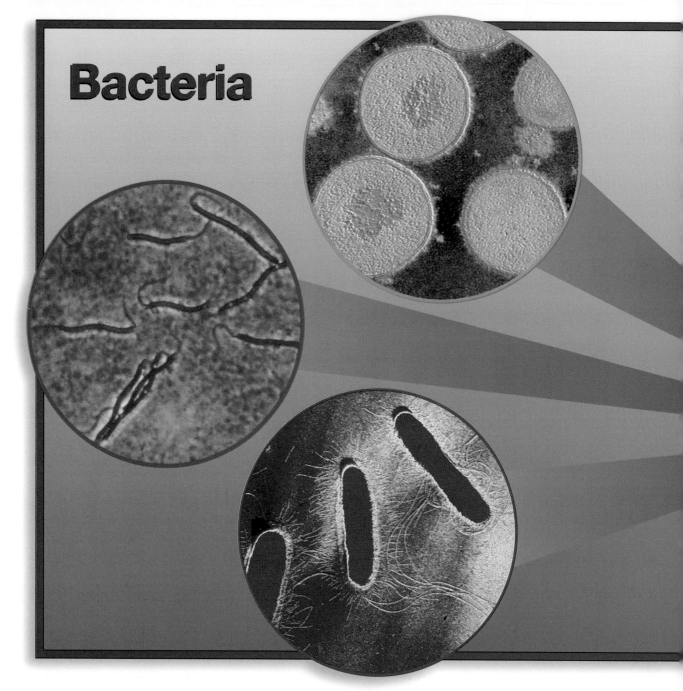

Looking at Germs

Germs can get inside your body. They can make you sick. Bacteria and viruses are two kinds of germs. Different germs cause different sicknesses.

Bacteria are very small living things. Bacteria cause some kinds of sore throats. If you do not brush your teeth, bacteria can cause tooth decay.

WHAT MAKES ME SICK

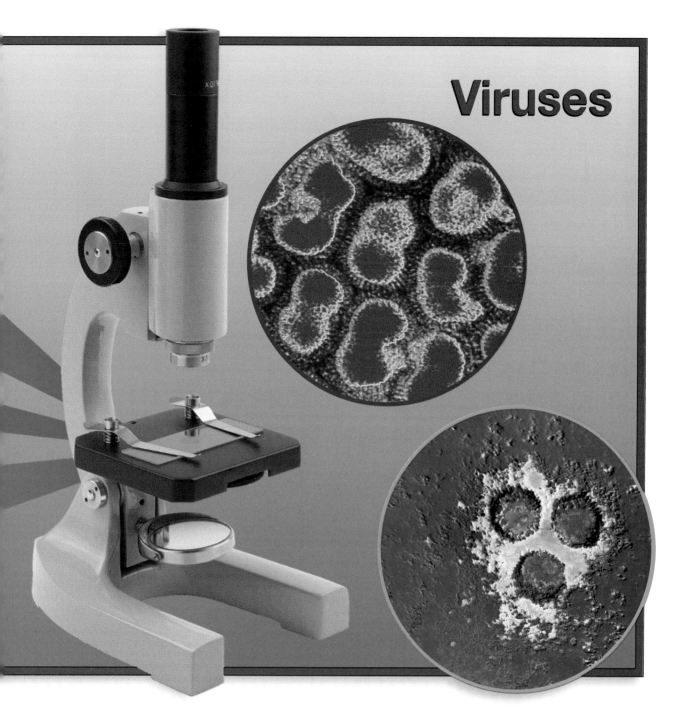

Viruses

Viruses grow inside living things. They cause colds and flu. Another virus causes chickenpox.

Germs are very small. A **microscope** helps you see things that are very small. The picture shows what some germs look like under a microscope. You need a very powerful microscope to see a virus.

Reading Check Tell about two kinds of germs and how they are alike and different.

How does a sneeze spread germs?

Activity
Examining a Pretend Sneeze

What You Need

sheet of plastic

tissues

paper towel

spray bottle of water

tape

Science Notebook

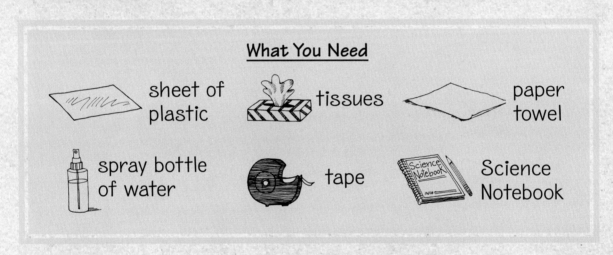

1 Tape a sheet of plastic to a wall. Spray water on the plastic. **Record** what you see.

2 Use a paper towel to dry the plastic.

3 Hold a tissue between the spray bottle and the plastic. Spray water on the tissue.

4 **Record** what you see. **Compare** your results.

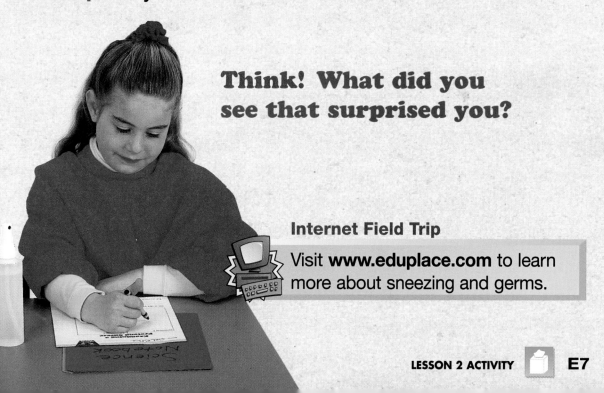

Think! What did you see that surprised you?

Internet Field Trip

Visit **www.eduplace.com** to learn more about sneezing and germs.

Sneezing Spreads Germs

The picture shows a boy sneezing. It begins with the boy throwing back his head. It ends with the boy sneezing into his hands. As he **sneezes**, air and liquid come out of his nose and mouth. There are germs in the liquid. The large circle shows how these germs look under a microscope.

What are some ways to keep germs from spreading when you sneeze? You can cover your nose and mouth with your hands. You can also hold a tissue over your nose and mouth. Remember to put the tissue in the trash. Then use soap and water to wash the germs off your hands.

Reading Check Write about how a sneeze spreads germs.

What are other ways that germs are spread?

Activity

Examining How Germs Travel

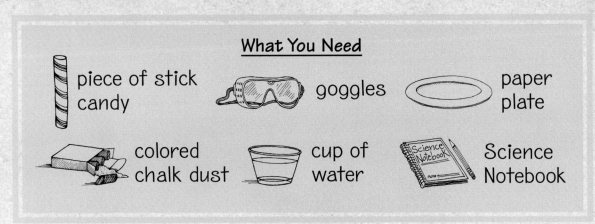

What You Need

piece of stick candy

goggles

paper plate

colored chalk dust

cup of water

Science Notebook

Science Notebook

1 Dip a piece of candy in water and roll it in chalk dust on a plate.

2 Roll the candy in your hands.

3 **Predict** what will happen when you shake hands with a classmate. **Record** your prediction.

Examining How Germs Travel	
Prediction	**Result**

4 Shake hands with a classmate. **Record** what happened.

Think! If the chalk dust were germs, in what other ways could germs be spread?

Germs Everywhere

Think about places where you might find germs.
Germs can be found almost everywhere. All of the
objects in this picture may have germs on them.

Arrows point to places where germs might be.
There may be germs on the paper, the eraser, and
the pencil. Where else might there be germs?

In the circles you see germs as you would see them under a microscope. The germs look bigger than they really are. Remember, germs are very small.

How might these objects have been covered with germs? A boy with germs on his hands touches the pencil. The germs **spread** to the pencil. Then when another boy touches the same pencil, the germs spread to his hands.

Even though you cannot see germs, you know they are there. How are these children spreading germs?

You know that germs might come from the hands of people when they touch objects. Germs may also come from people who sneeze near objects. If a child sneezes or coughs, germs may spray onto the objects. Then when someone touches the same object, the germs spread to that person's hands.

WHAT MAKES ME SICK

What are some ways you can keep germs from spreading? You can wash your hands. You can wash things that are touched by many hands. You can cover your nose and mouth with a tissue when you sneeze or cough. You can also keep things that don't belong in your mouth out of your mouth.

✔ Reading Check **Draw a picture** that shows two ways children can spread germs.

4 How does your body protect you from germs?

Activity

Examining How Dust Collects

What You Need

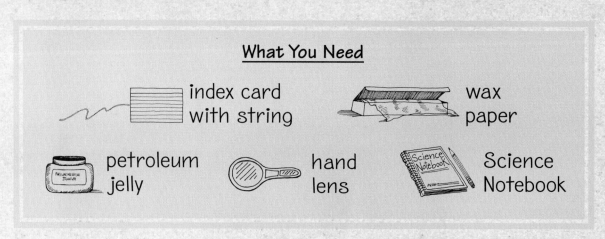

index card with string

wax paper

petroleum jelly

hand lens

Science Notebook

① Use wax paper to spread petroleum jelly on an index card.

2 **Observe** the index card with a hand lens. **Record** what you see.

3 Hang the card where moving air will blow on it.

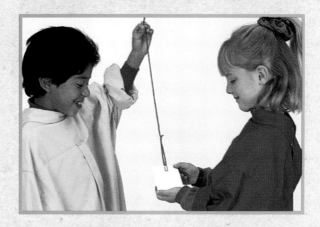

4 *Using Math* Repeat step 2 after two days. **Compare** your results.

Think! Why did the surface of the card change?

Find Out More!

Use a microscope to look at the index cards from all the groups. Which card has the most dust? What does that tell you about germs?

Trapping Germs

Look at the picture of the girl playing baseball. She is kicking up dust as she slides. What are the other children doing? They are also putting dust into the air.

Think about how it feels to breathe when dust is in the air. Dust can make it hard to breathe. Dust has germs in it. So dust puts germs into the air.

Your body protects you from germs. One way is by trapping dust and germs in mucus. **Mucus** is a sticky material in your nose, mouth, and throat.

Mucus helps trap dust and germs to keep them from getting farther into your body. Germs cannot make you sick if they cannot get into your body.

Reading Check Tell about one way that your body protects you from germs.

UNIT E CHECKPOINT

Word Power

If you need help, turn to the pages shown in blue.

Match a word with a picture. (E4–E5) (E8–E9)

microscope   sneeze   germs

1. 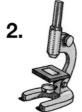 2.  3.

Use these words to fill in the blanks.

bacteria   mucus   spread   virus

4. When you pick up an object, germs _____ to your hands. (E12–E13)

5. Small living things that can cause a sore throat are called _____. (E4–E5)

6. A sticky material in your nose, mouth, and throat is called _____. (E18–E19)

7. The germ that causes a cold is called a _____. (E4–E5)

Solving Science Problems

The children in your class keep getting sick. Explain why you think this happens. What are some things you and your classmates can do to stay healthy? Make a plan. Share your plan with your classmates.

People Using Science

Lab Technician

When you have a sore throat, a doctor may use a swab to get some germs from your throat. The doctor sends the germs to a lab technician.

A lab technician looks at the germs under a microscope. Then he or she tells the doctor what kind of germs they are.

Why is it helpful to know what kind of germs are in your throat?

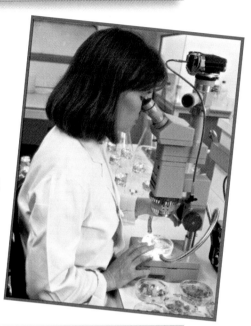

 Guess and Check

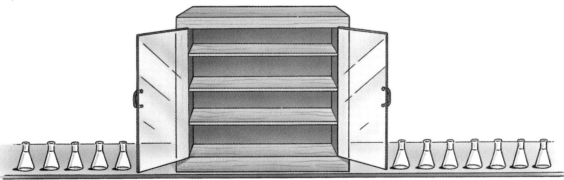

Guess and then use counters to check each answer.

1. Mr. Ortiz has 12 bottles. There are 4 shelves in the cabinet. He wants to put the same number of bottles on each shelf. How many bottles should he put on each shelf?

2. If there were only 3 shelves, how many bottles should Mr. Ortiz put on each shelf?

How can you prevent the spread of germs?

Activity

Stopping Germs From Spreading

What You Need

Science Notebook

1 **Talk** to your school nurse about germs and how they are spread.

2 **Find** places in school where germs might be spread. **Record** what you observe.

Stopping Germs From Spreading	
Where germs are spread	My plan

3 **Make a plan** to help stop the spread of germs in school.

4 **Record** your plan. Then carry out your plan.

Think! How could you prevent germs from spreading in your home?

Internet Field Trip

Visit **www.eduplace.com** to learn more about ways germs spread.

Protect Yourself

Think about how germs might be spread in each picture. The first boy has cut his knee. Germs can get inside his body through the cut. The girls are drinking from the same straw. They are sharing germs. The last boy is about to pick up an apple core. It carries the germs of the person who ate it.

What can be done to keep germs from spreading? The first boy can wash the cut with soap and water. Then he can put a bandage on the cut to keep it clean. Each girl should have her own drink.

The last boy should use a napkin or paper towel to pick up the apple core. He should throw it away in the trash. Then the boy should wash his hands with soap and water.

All of these people are helping to keep germs from spreading.

◀ This girl is washing her hands with soap and water. She is killing the germs on her skin.

This boy washed his cut with soap and water. His mom puts a bandage on it to keep germs out. ▶

◀ This girl keeps her mouth away from the spout. This helps keep germs that are on the spout out of her body.

WHAT MAKES ME SICK

This man is cleaning away germs. He uses a **disinfectant** to help kill the germs. ▼

Decide if each of the four activities shown takes less than one minute or more than one minute. Record your ideas in a chart like the one below.

Keeping Germs From Spreading	
Less than one minute	**More than one minute**

✓ **Reading Check Act out a story** that shows one way that you can keep germs from spreading.

LESSON 6

How can you prevent sickness and injury?

Activity

Examining Health and Safety

What You Need

 crayons

 Science Notebook

1 Look at the cartoon strip. **Tell** what happens first, next, and last.

2 **Draw** your own cartoon strip in a chart. First, show someone who is sick or injured.

3 Next, show what could be done to make that person healthy again.

4 Last, show how the sickness or injury could have been prevented.

Think! What can you do at home to prevent sickness and injury?

Examining Health and Safety	
First	
Next	
Last	

Preventing Injury

Look at the picture story. What happened? One of the boys hit his head on the sidewalk. He has a head **injury**. Why does one boy have a head injury but the other boy does not? The boy that hurt his head was not wearing a **safety helmet**. The boy without the injury was wearing a safety helmet.

WHAT MAKES ME SICK

The boy who hurt his head can **prevent**, or stop, an injury from happening again. The most important way is to wear a safety helmet.

What else can the boy do to prevent an injury? He can pedal slower. He can be careful to watch where he is going. The boy might even wear elbow pads on his arms and kneepads on his legs. These pads will protect the boy if he falls.

There are many things that you can do to prevent injury. Be careful near the street. Only cross when it is safe. Look both ways to make sure there are no cars. Look for the walk sign if there is one.

When you carry sharp objects, you should walk slowly. You should keep the point away from you and others. When passing scissors, hold the blades and point the handle toward the other person.

WHAT MAKES ME SICK

You can help prevent injuries when playing sports. A hockey player wears a safety helmet, pads, and special gloves for protection.

You can help prevent injuries when riding in a car. You should stay seated. You should always wear a **seat belt**. Young children should ride in car seats.

> ✅ **Reading Check** **Write a story** about someone who prevents an injury from happening.

LESSON 7

How can you stay healthy?

Activity

Exploring Healthful Activities

What You Need

pictures of healthful activities

crayons

Science Notebook

1 **Look at** some pictures of healthful activities. **Talk about** why the activities are healthful.

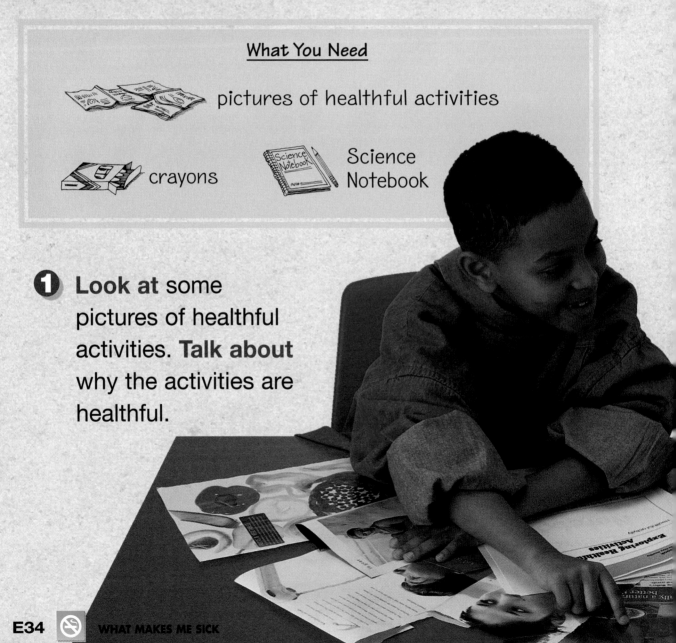

2 Think of another healthful activity.

3 **Draw** a picture of yourself doing that activity.

4 **Write** about how your activity will help you stay healthy.

Think! What are some other ways you can keep your body healthy?

Find Out More!

What else do you want to know about staying healthy? Ask questions. Make a plan to find answers. Share your findings with your classmates.

Staying Healthy

How can you keep your body healthy? You can eat **healthful foods**. These kinds of foods help your body grow strong. You can also **exercise**. This will make your muscles and bones stronger.

Getting enough sleep helps keep you healthy, too. When you sleep, your body gets the rest it needs.

Too many cookies, candies, or potato chips are not good for you. Alcohol, cigarettes, and drugs are not good for you either.

Follow the maze with your finger. Decide which things are good for your body. You will get to the finish by choosing healthful things.

Reading Check **Draw a picture** to show three ways that you can help your body stay healthy.

Word Power

If you need help, turn to the pages shown in blue.

Match the words with a picture. (E30–E33)

injury   safety helmet   seat belt

1.    **2.**    **3.**

Write the letter of the correct words.

4. You wear a safety helmet to _____ an injury. (E30–E31)
  a. prevent   **b.** sneeze   **c.** spread   **d.** exercise

5. A _____ helps you see things that are small. (E4–E5)
  a. injury   **b.** sneeze   **c.** germ   **d.** microscope

6. A _____ helps to kill germs. (E26–E27)
  a. mucus   **b.** seat belt   **c.** injury   **d.** disinfectant

7. Bacteria and viruses are two kinds of _____. (E4–E5)
  a. germs   **b.** exercises   **c.** mucus   **d.** injuries

8. A sticky material that helps keep germs from getting into your body is called _____. (E18–E19)
  a. seat belt   **b.** bacteria   **c.** mucus   **d.** disinfectant

9. You _____ to make your muscles stronger. (E36–E37)
  a. spread   **b.** exercise   **c.** prevent   **d.** sneeze

10. You should eat _____ to help your body grow. (E36–E37)
  a. seat belts   **b.** viruses   **c.** bacteria   **d.** healthful foods

Using Science Ideas

How are germs being spread? Make a list.

Writing in Science

Explain how each action helps keep you and others healthy. Share your ideas with your classmates.

1. Washing hands

2. Wearing a safety helmet

3. Using a disinfectant

4. Using a tissue when you sneeze

5. Eating fruit instead of chips

Make a poster. Use words and pictures to show ways to stay healthy.

Main Idea and Details

Matthew likes to keep germs from spreading. When he sneezes, Matthew covers his mouth and nose with a tissue. He puts the tissue in the trash. Then he washes his hands with soap and water. When Matthew gets a cut, he washes it. Then his mother covers the cut with a bandage.

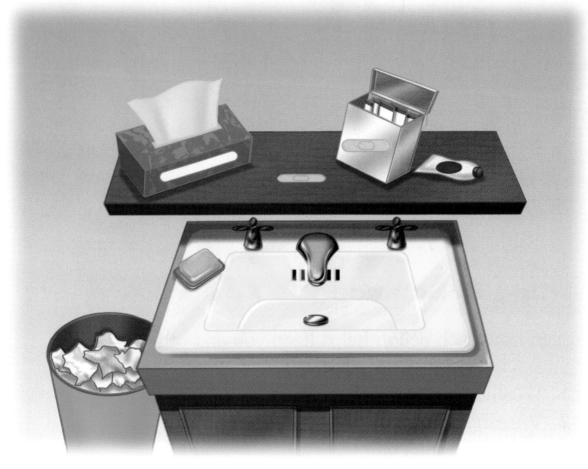

Use the story above to answer the questions.

   1. What is the main idea of the story?

   2. What are three things that Matthew does to help keep germs from spreading?

Find a Pattern

Find each pattern.

1. Alan does sit-ups to stay healthy. On Tuesday he does 5. On Wednesday he does 10. On Thursday he does 15. What is the pattern?

2. Tanya roller-skates to exercise. On her first try, she roller-skates for 10 minutes. On her second try, she skates for 20 minutes. On her third try, she skates for 30 minutes. What is the pattern?

3. Marco does jumping jacks to stay healthy. On Monday he does 7 jumping jacks. On Tuesday he does 17. On Wednesday he does 27. What is the pattern? If he continues this pattern, how many jumping jacks will Marco do on Thursday?

SCIENCE and MATH TOOLBOX

Using a
Hand Lens

A hand lens is a tool that makes objects look bigger. It helps you see the small parts of an object.

Look at a Coin

1. Place a coin on your desk.

2. Hold the hand lens above the coin. Look through the lens. Slowly move the lens away from the coin. What do you see?

3. Keep moving the lens away until the coin looks blurry.

4. Then slowly move the lens closer. Stop when the coin does not look blurry.

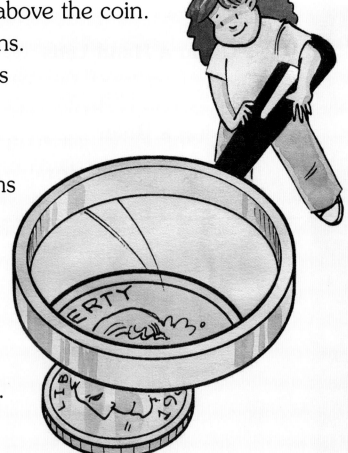

Using a
Thermometer

A thermometer is a tool used to measure temperature. Temperature tells how hot or cold something is. It is measured in degrees.

Find the Temperature of Water

1. Put water into a cup.

2. Put a thermometer into the cup.

3. Watch the colored liquid in the thermometer. What do you see?

4. Look how high the colored liquid is. What number is closest? That is the temperature of the water.

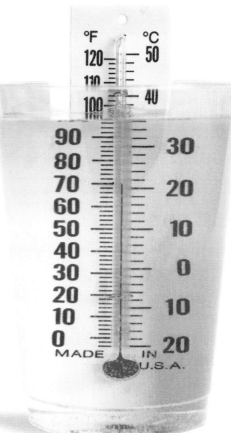

Using a
Ruler

A ruler is a tool used to measure the length of objects. Some rulers measure length in inches. Other rulers measure length in centimeters.

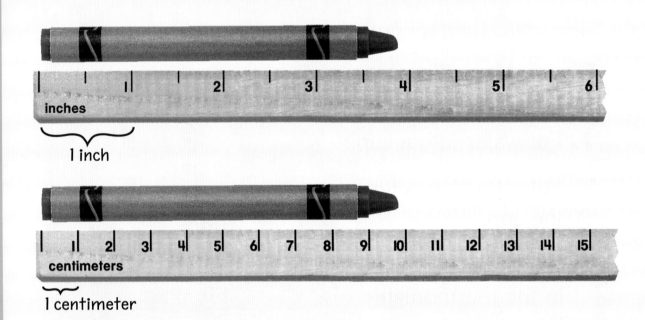

1 inch

1 centimeter

Measure a Crayon

1. Place the ruler on your desk.

2. Lay your crayon next to the ruler. Line up one end with the 0 mark on the ruler.

3. Look at the other end of the crayon. Which number is closest to that end?

Using a
Calculator

A calculator is a tool that can help you add numbers. It can also help you subtract numbers.

Subtract Numbers

1. Tim and Anna both grew plants.
Tim grew 8 plants.
Anna grew 17 plants.

2. How many more plants did Anna grow?
Use your calculator to find out.

3. Enter [1] [7] on the calculator.
Then press the [−] key.
Enter [8] and press [=].

4. What is your answer?

Using a Balance

A balance is a tool used to measure mass. Mass is the amount of matter in an object.

Measure the Mass of Clay

1. Check that the pointer is on the middle mark of the balance. If needed, move the slider on the back to the left or right.

2. Place a clay ball in one pan.

3. Add masses to the other pan until the pointer is at the middle mark again.

4. Add the numbers on the masses to find the mass in grams of the clay.

5. Add more clay to the ball. Repeat steps 3 and 4. How did the mass change?

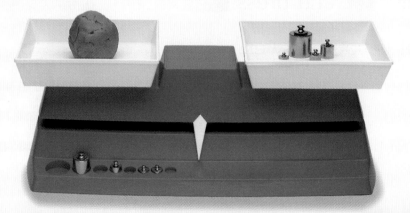

Making a Chart

A chart can help you sort information, or data. When you sort data it is easier to read and compare.

Make a Chart to Compare Animals

1. Give the chart a title.

2. Name the groups that tell about the data you collect.

3. Carefully fill in the data in each column.

How Animals Move	
Animal	**How it moves**
fish	swim
dog	walk, swim
duck	walk, swim, fly

Which animal can move in the most ways?

Making a Tally Chart

A tally chart helps you keep track of items as you count.

Make a Tally Chart of Kinds of Pets

Jan's class drew pictures of their pets. You can make a tally chart to record the number of each kind of pet.

1. Every time you count one pet, you make one tally.

2. When you get to five, your fifth tally should be a line across the other four.

3. Count the tallies to find each total.

Kinds of Pets		
Pet	**Tally**	**Total**
Bird	III	3
Dog	IIII I	6
Fish	I	1

How many of each kind of pet do the children have?

Making a Bar Graph

A bar graph can help you sort and compare data.

Make a Bar Graph of Favorite Leaves

You can use the data in the tally chart to make a bar graph.

Favorite Leaves		
Leaf	Tally	Total
Oak	IIII	4
Ash	IIII I	6
Maple	II	2
Birch	III	3

1. Choose a title for your graph.

2. Write numbers along the side.

3. Write leaf names along the bottom.

4. Start at the bottom of each column. Fill in one box for each tally.

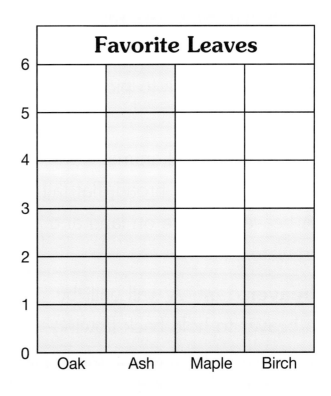

Favorite Leaves

Which leaf is the favorite?

GLOSSARY

B

bacteria Tiny living things that can only be seen with a microscope. Some bacteria cause sickness. (E4)

beak The jaws of a bird along with their hard coverings. A bird uses its beak to pick up food. (A26)

beaver A small animal with brown fur and a broad, flat tail. A beaver can live on land and in water. (A34)

beaver dam A wall built by a beaver to hold back flowing water. A beaver dam is made with cut trees, stones, and mud. (A34)

bill A bird's beak. A pelican uses its bill to scoop up and store fish. (A26)

C

condense To change from a gas to a liquid. When water vapor in the air cools, it condenses to form clouds. (D41)

D

dinosaur An animal that lived millions of years ago. All dinosaurs lived on land. (C4)

disinfectant A material that kills germs. Cleaning with a disinfectant helps prevent the spread of germs. (E27)

E

environment All the living and nonliving things that are around a living thing. A drop of water, a rotting log, a desert, an ocean, and a rain forest are different kinds of environments. (A40)

erosion The washing away of the land. The roots of trees can help stop erosion. (A41)

evaporate To change from a liquid to a gas. Water evaporates to form water vapor. (D37)

exercise Moving your body. Playing outdoors is *exercise* that helps make your muscles and bones stronger. (E36)

extinct When all animals of one kind die. There are no dinosaurs today because these animals are extinct. (C5)

F

flat teeth Teeth that are good for grinding food. Most plant-eating dinosaurs had flat teeth. (C23)

force A push or a pull. A force can cause an object to move, stop, or change direction. (B24)

fossil remains What is left of a plant or an animal that lived long ago. (C18)

freeze To change from a liquid to a solid. Water freezes into ice at a temperature of 32°F. (D47)

G

gas A form of matter that does not have a set shape. A gas spreads out to fill what it is in. (D20)

germ A tiny living thing that can make you sick. Bacteria and viruses are two kinds of germs. (E4)

gravity A force that pulls objects toward the earth. When a frog jumps, gravity pulls it back down to the earth. (B27)

H

habitat A place in which a plant or an animal lives. In its habitat a living thing gets all the things it needs. (A8)

healthful foods Foods that are good for your body. Fruits, vegetables, breads, milk, and fish are healthful foods. (E36)

heat A form of energy used to change matter. Heat is used to warm homes. Heat can change a solid to a liquid. (B42, D31)

I

injury Something harmful that happens to a person. Some injuries are cuts, scrapes, bruises, and broken bones. (E30)

L

leaves Parts of a plant that grow on a stem or grow up from roots. Leaves make food. (A13)

lens A piece of transparent glass or plastic that brings together or spreads rays of light. A lens can make an object look bigger or smaller. (B16)

light A form of energy that you can see. Light from a flashlight travels in a straight line. (B4)

liquid Matter that takes the shape of its container. Grape juice is a liquid. (D10)

living thing Something that is alive and can grow. Living things need food, water, and air. (A4)

lodge A beaver's home. A lodge has underwater entrances and a dry room inside. (A36)

matter What all things are made of. All matter takes up space. (D4)

melt To change from a solid to a liquid. When ice melts, it changes to liquid water. (D32)

microscope A tool that makes small things appear larger. Most germs can be seen with the aid of a microscope. (E5)

motion Moving from one place to another. When something is in motion, it changes its position. (B20)

mucus A sticky material that traps germs and dust. Mucus in your nose, mouth, and throat help protect your body from germs. (E19)

natural resource A material found in or on the earth that people use. Water, oil, gas, and trees are natural resources. (B46)

nonliving thing Something that was never alive. A rock is a nonliving thing. (A5)

once-living thing Something that was alive at one time or was once part of a living thing. A log is an example of a once-living thing. (A5)

opaque Keeping light from passing through. An opaque object casts a shadow. The human body and a paper bag are both opaque. (B10)

phases The apparent changes in the shape of the moon as seen from the earth. The pattern of the phases of the moon takes about 28 days. (C35)

pitch How high or low a sound is. The pitch of a gong is low. (B36)

pointed teeth Sharp teeth that are good for tearing food. Most meat-eating dinosaurs had pointed teeth. (C23)

prevent To keep from happening. Wearing a safety helmet when skating can help prevent injury. (E31)

reflect To throw back. A mirror reflects light. The moon reflects the light of the sun. (B6, C34)

resource Anything that plants or animals use to live. (A19)

riverbed The area where water flows between the sides of a river. A beaver builds its dam across a riverbed to stop the water. (A34)

root The part of a plant that grows down into the soil. Roots hold the plant in place and soak up water and minerals. (A13)

rotate To turn around a center point or an axis. The earth rotates once every 24 hours. (C31)

safety helmet
A hard covering to protect the head. It is a good idea to wear a safety helmet when riding a bike. (E30)

seat belt
A strap to hold a person in place while riding in a car. Wearing a seat belt can help prevent injuries. (E33)

shadow
A dark shape formed when an object blocks light. Shadows can change when the object moves. (B13)

shelter
A place where an animal can rest and be safe. An animal stores food and raises its young in a shelter. (A22)

skeleton
The bones of the body that hold up the body and help it move. Scientists have found dinosaur skeletons. (C12)

skull
The bones that shape the head and protect the brain. The skull includes the bones of the face and jaw. (C24)

sneeze
A sudden forcing of breath through the nose and mouth. Sneezing is one way that germs are spread. (E8)

solid
A form of matter that has its own shape. When a solid is put into a jar, the shape of the solid stays the same. (D4)

sound
Waves of vibration that you hear. Waves vibrate faster for high sounds than for low sounds. (B33)

speed How fast an object moves. The speed of a dog running is greater than the speed of a turtle walking. (B21)

spine A tiny, sharp leaf of a cactus. Spines protect a cactus from being eaten by animals. (A14)

spread To pass from one person to another. Diseases are spread by sneezing, coughing, and touching objects that have germs on them. (E13)

stem The supporting and connecting part of a plant. Water and food move through stems. (A13)

sunrise The daily appearance of the sun in the eastern sky as the earth turns to face the sun. The sky becomes light at sunrise. (C31)

sunset The daily disappearance of the sun in the western sky as the earth turns away from the sun. The sky becomes dark after sunset. (C31)

texture The way something feels. Rough and smooth are textures. (D5)

trace fossil The imprint of a once-living thing. Dinosaur footprints in rock are one kind of trace fossil. (C19)

translucent Allowing some light to pass through. Some translucent objects are frosted glass and waxed paper. (B10)

transparent Allowing light to pass through. Clear water and plastic wrap are transparent. (B10)

---

vibration Fast motion back and forth. You can see the vibration of a guitar string if you pluck it. (B32)

virus A very small germ that causes sickness. You need a very powerful microscope to see a virus. (E5)

volume The loudness of a sound. The volume control on a telephone can be used to make the volume louder or softer. (B37)

---

water cycle The changes that happen to water in nature. The steps of the water cycle are (1) water evaporates, (2) water condenses to form clouds, (3) water falls as rain, and (4) water evaporates again. (D42)

water vapor Water that is a gas. You cannot see water vapor. (D37)

wave An up-and-down or back-and-forth motion. Water moves in waves on the ocean. Sound moves in waves through the air. (B32)

SAYING DINOSAUR NAMES

Albertosaurus al bur tuh SAWR us

Allosaurus al oh SAWR us

Apatosaurus uh pat uh SAWR us

Brachiosaurus brak ee uh SAWR us

Compsognathus kahmp SAHG nuh thus

Corythosaurus kawr ihnth uh SAWR us

Diplodocus dih PLAHD uh kus

Edmontosaurus ed mahn tuh SAWR us

Lambeosaurus lam bee oh SAWR us

Ornitholestes awr nih thuh LES teez

Seismosaurus syz muh SAWR us

Stegosaurus steg uh SAWR us

Styracosaurus stihr uh koh SAWR us

Triceratops trye SER uh tahps

Tyrannosaurus tuh ran uh SAWR us

Velociraptor vuh LAHS uh rap tur

INDEX

A

Air
  as a gas, D18–D20, D24, D40
  temperature, C38–C39, C42–C43, C45, C47
  trapping, D18–D19
  and water vapor, D40–D42
Albertosaurus, C23–C25
Alcohol, E37
Allosaurus, C4–C5
Aloe, A44–A45
Animals
  body parts, A26–A29
  desert, A8, A46–A47
  needs of, A4, A8–A9, A17, A19, A37
  shelter, A20–A23, A36, A47
Apatosaurus, C7
Arctic, A50–A51

B

Bacteria, E4
Beak, A26–A27, C24
Beaver, A32–A36
Beaver dam, A32–A36
Big Dipper, C36–C37
Bill, A26, C24
Bones, E36
  digging for, C10–C11
  of dinosaurs, C12–C13, C15, C18
Brachiosaurus, C4–C5, C9
Burning, and heat, B43

C

Cactus, A14–A15, A44–A47
California, weather in, C47
Changes
  in animal habitats, A34–A37
  in dinosaur remains, C18–C19

CREDITS

ILLUSTRATORS
Cover Ruth Flanigan.

Think Like a Scientist 2–7: Steven Carpenter. 10–11: Laurie Hamilton. *border* Ruth Flanigan.

Unit A 13,15: Dan McGowan. 22–23: Debbie Pinkney Davis. 30: Tom Pansini. 34–37: Bob Pepper. 50–51: Geosystems. 52: Tom Pansini. 54: Shelly Dieterichs.

Unit B 4–7: John Ceballos. 28–29: Tom Pansini. 36–39: Tate Nation. 42–43: Mike Dammer. 48: Tom Pansini. 49: Mike Dammer. 51: Patrick Girouard.

Unit C C: Phil Wilson. 1: Dan Hubig. 4–5: Richard Courtney. 6–7: Robert Frank. 8–9, 22–25: Phil Wilson. 26: Tom Pansini. 27: Phil Wilson. 30–31: Dan Hubig. 34–35: Jim Durk. 36–37: Tom Powers. 48: Tom Pansini. 50: Shelley Dieterichs.

Unit D D: *t.* Robert Roper, *b.* Tom Pansini. 1: Tom Pansini, Terry Taylor. 26: Tom Pansini. 27: Argus. 42–43: Robert Roper. 46–47: Terry Taylor. 50–51: Brian Karas. 52: Tom Pansini. 54: Elise Mills.

Unit E 20–21: Tom Pansini. 28–29: Eldon Doty. 30–31: Jerry Zimmerman. 36–37: Jenny Campbell. 38–39: Tom Pansini. 40–41: Mark McIntyre.

Science and Math Toolbox *logos* Nancy Tobin. 5: Randy Verougstraete. 7–8: Randy Chewning. 10: Randy Verougstraete. *border* Ruth Flanigan.

Glossary 10–18 Tom Pansini.

PHOTOGRAPHS
All photographs by Houghton Mifflin Company (HMCo.) unless otherwise noted.

Cover *t.* David Phillips/Visuals Unlimited; *m.l.* Picture Perfect USA; *b.r.* Guy Grenier/Masterfile Corporation.

Unit A A: *m.l.* Tony Stone Images; *m.r.* Charles Krebs/Tony Stone Images. 1: *m.l.* Zefa Germany/The Stock Market; *m.r.* Tom Tietz/Tony Stone Images. 4–5: Randy Wells/Allstock/Tony Stone Images. 5: *t.* Dwight Kuhn/DRK Photo; *b.* Leonard Lee Rue III/ Bruce Coleman Incorporated. 8: Laurence Hughes/The Image Bank. 9: Pat O'Hara/Tony Stone Images. 12: Runk/Schoenberger/Grant Heilman Photography, Inc. 14: Runk/Schoenberger/Grant Heilman Photography, Inc. 18–19: James Randklev/Tony Stone Images. 26: *t.l.* William J. Weber/Visuals Unlimited; *b.l.* Darrell Gulin/Tony Stone Images. 26–27: *t.* Zefa Germany/The Stock Market; *b.* © Francois Gohier/Photo Researchers, Inc. 27: *t.* Zefa Germany/The Stock Market; *b.* Tom Tietz/Tony Stone Images. 28: *t.l.* Tom & Pat Leeson/Leeson Photography; *b.l.* Tui De Roy/Bruce Coleman Incorporated. 29: *t.* Raymond A. Mendez/Animals Animals/Earth Scenes; *b.* John Cancalosi/DRK Photo. 31: David R. Frazier Photography. 35: *t.* © Tom & Pat Leeson/Photo Researchers, Inc.; *m.* Tom Mangelson/Images of Nature; *b.* Johnny Johnson/Animals Animals/Earth Scenes. 37: *t.* Peter Ward/Bruce Coleman Incorporated; *b.* Norman Owen Tomalin/Bruce Coleman Incorporated. 42: *t.* Superstock; *b.* Superstock. 43: Thomas Kitchin/Tom Stack & Associates. 46–47: Gabe Palmer/The Stock Market. 47: *t.* John Cancalosi/Stock Boston; *b.* © Jerry L. Ferrara/Photo Researchers, Inc. 50: Tony Stone Images. 50–51: *r.* Charles Krebs/Tony Stone Images. 53: Erwin & Peggy Bauer/Bruce Coleman Incorporated.

Unit B B: *l.* John De Visser/Masterfile Corporation; *r.* Richard V. Procopio/Stock Boston. 1: Jerome Prevost-TempSport/Corbis Corporation. 10–11: Superstock. 12–13: Superstock. 20: *t.* B. Daemmrich/The Image Works Incorporated. 20–21: *bkgd.* PhotoDisc, Inc; *inset* Jerome Prevost-TempSport/Corbis Corporation. 21: *l.* Neil Preston/Corbis Corporation; *r.* Luongo/The Gamma Liaison Network. 26: *t.* Phil Degginger/Color-Pic, Inc.; *m.* E.R. Degginger/Color-Pic, Inc.; *b.* Matt Bradley/Tom Stack & Associates. 27: Jack Vartoogian Photography. 32: *inset* James H. Karales/Peter Arnold, Inc. 33: *bkgd.* Richard Gross/The Stock Market; *inset* Richard Gross/The Stock Market. 46: *b.l.* Anthony Redpath/The Stock Market; *b.r.* John De Visser/Masterfile Corporation. 47: *b.* Richard V. Procopio/Stock Boston.

Unit C 18: © Francois Gohier/Photo Researchers, Inc. 19: *l.* Tom & Susan Bean, Inc. 25: © Tom McHugh/Photo Researchers, Inc. 27: Stephen Trimble/DRK Photo. 36–37: Anselm Spring/The Image Bank. 40–41: Tom & Therisa Stack/Tom Stack & Associates. 46: Gabe Palmer/The Stock Market. 47: Richard R. Hansen. 49: Louis

Extra Practice

On the following pages are questions about each of the Units in your book. Use these questions to help you review some of the terms and ideas that you studied. Write your answers on a separate sheet of paper.

Contents

Extra Practice

Word Power

Match each living thing with its habitat.

woodland   swamp   desert

1.   **2.**   **3.**

Use these words to answer the riddles.

roots   stems   spines   leaves

4. We help protect a cactus from animals.

5. We carry water and food to other parts of the plant.

6. We take in water and minerals from the soil.

7. We use sunlight to make food for the plant.

Write the letter of the correct words.

8. A place where animals can be warm and safe is a _____.
   a. living thing   **b.** spine   **c.** erosion   **d.** shelter

9. The roots of a tree can stop _____.
   a. environments   **b.** deserts   **c.** erosion   **d.** habitats

10. Trash dumped into a river is harmful to the _____.
   a. nonliving things   **b.** environment   **c.** erosion   **d.** shelter

Extra Practice

Using Science Ideas

Write each answer.

1. Make a chart like the one shown. Sort these items into living things, once-living things, and nonliving things.

Living Things	Once-Living Things	Nonliving Things

2. Name two ways beavers change their habitat.

3. Name some ways birds use their beaks.

4. Name some ways a shelter helps an animal.

Extra Practice

UNIT B Energy and Motion

Word Power

Use these words to fill in the blanks.

shadow   transparent   translucent   opaque

1. Light does not pass through _____ objects.
2. If you stand in front of a light, you make a _____.
3. Light passes through _____ objects.
4. Objects that let some light through are _____.

Write the letter of the answer to the riddle.

5. I tell the loudness of sound.
   a. vibration   **b.** pitch   **c.** volume   **d.** gravity

6. I am a wave that you can hear.
   a. gravity   **b.** volume   **c.** sound   **d.** motion

7. I tell how high or low a sound is.
   a. pitch   **b.** volume   **c.** speed   **d.** shadow

8. I am the force that pulls you toward the earth.
   a. vibration   **b.** gravity   **c.** wave   **d.** motion

9. I tell how fast an animal can run.
   a. gravity   **b.** speed   **c.** motion   **d.** pitch

10. I am a back-and-forth motion.
    a. vibration   **b.** pitch   **c.** shadow   **d.** volume

Extra Practice

Using Science Ideas

Write each answer.

1. Order these sounds from softest to loudest.

2. How can you tell if a ball is in motion?

3. Name some ways that heat is made.

4. In what ways can forces change an object's motion?

Extra Practice

Word Power

Match each word with a picture.

phases   reflects   rotates

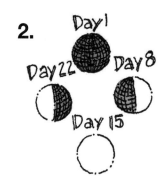

Use these words to fill in the blanks.

skull   trace fossils   flat teeth   fossil remains

4. Most plant-eating dinosaurs had _____.

5. Dinosaur footprints found in rock are _____.

6. Rocks called _____ were once dinosaur bones.

7. The head of a skeleton is the _____.

Write the letter of the correct word.

8. The earth turns, or _____, every 24 hours.
   a. rises   **b.** sets   **c.** phases   **d.** rotates

9. As the earth turns away from the sun, you see a _____.
   a. sunrise   **b.** sunset   **c.** phase   **d.** season

10. A dinosaur's _____ shows its size and shape.
   a. skeleton   **b.** tooth   **c.** extinct   **d.** phase

Using Science Ideas

Write each answer.

1. What can you tell about these two dinosaurs?

2. Why do stars seem to move during the night?

3. How big were dinosaurs?

4. Describe how the moon changes from night to night.

UNIT D Solids, Liquids, and Gases

Word Power

Match each word with a picture.

evaporate   melt   condense

1.

2.

3.

Write the letter of the correct words.

4. A _____ takes the shape of its container.
a. solid   **b.** matter   **c.** liquid   **d.** texture

5. The changes from river water to clouds to rain show
a _____.
a. water cycle   **b.** liquid   **c.** solid   **d.** texture

6. To change a crayon from a solid to a liquid, add _____.
a. texture   **b.** heat   **c.** matter   **d.** rain

7. Cat fur has a soft _____.
a. liquid   **b.** heat   **c.** texture   **d.** matter

8. A _____ stays the same size and shape.
a. liquid   **b.** gas   **c.** solid   **d.** matter

9. Solids, liquids, and gases are made of _____.
a. matter   **b.** heat   **c.** water vapor   **d.** air

10. The air around you is a mixture of _____.
a. textures   **b.** solids   **c.** liquids   **d.** gases

Extra Practice

Using Science Ideas

Write each answer.

1. Tell about the changes shown in the pictures.

2. Name three ways you can group solids.
3. How are liquids and gases alike?
4. How does water from a river become water in clouds?

UNIT E What Makes Me Sick

Word Power

Match the words with a picture.

exercise   safety helmet   seat belt

1.

2.

3.

Use these words to answer the riddles.

bacteria   mucus   virus   healthful food

4. I am a sticky material inside your nose that traps dust and germs.

5. I am a germ that causes the flu.

6. I am a germ that causes tooth decay.

7. I help your body grow strong.

Write the letter of the correct words.

8. Your muscles and bones grow stronger when you _____.
   a. exercise   **b.** sneeze   **c.** injury   **d.** spread

9. You can use a _____ to kill germs.
   a. microscope **b.** disinfectant **c.** seat belt **d.** virus

10. A football player wears a helmet to prevent _____.
    a. germs   **b.** spread   **c.** exercise   **d.** injury

Extra Practice

Using Science Ideas

Write each answer.

1. How can you help prevent injuries when you go skating?

2. What can you do to keep germs from spreading when you sneeze?

3. Tell how to pass scissors to a friend.

4. Why is dust harmful?